HOLY INTIMACY

DWELLING WITH GOD IN THE SECRET PLACE

Lori Wagner

Holy Intimacy

Dwelling with God in the Secret Place

HOLY INTIMACY:
DWELLING WITH GOD IN THE SECRET PLACE

Requests for information should be addressed to:
Affirming Faith
1181 Whispering Knoll Lane
Rochester Hills, MI 48306
loriwagner@affirmingfaith.com
www.affirmingfaith.com
Printed in the United States of America.

This book is dedicated
with love and appreciation
to my husband,
Bill Wagner.

TABLE OF CONTENTS

INTRODUCTION

I t was New Years Eve 2009. My family and I were in church for a good old-fashioned "Watch Night" service. Part of the celebration included recognizing those who had read the Bible through the previous year, and I realized too many years had passed since my last journey through the holy pages.

January 2, I began. I was excited to be in the Word and easily made it through Genesis. I devoured the first 25 chapters of Exodus, and then something happened. My reading regimen was hijacked by the Holy Ghost.

As I read about the Tabernacle of Moses in the wilderness, its symbolism and beauty drew me into a curtained call to intimacy with God. I immediately launched into a full-blown study, fascinated by the Tabernacle's many intertwining elements and themes. What began as a simple devotional reading, grew into what I thought might result in an article or conference presentation, and then mushroomed into the work you now hold in your hands.

The main theme of this book, God's plan for intimacy as revealed in the Tabernacle of Moses, is contained in Chapters 1 through 13. Throughout the chapters you will find related tangent thoughts I found too interesting to keep to myself, and following the main text, appendices provide additional food for thought. Instead of detracting from the heart of the message, these side notes and appendices have been separated from the body of the book, but are included for those whose hearts, like mine, are enamored with the beauty and intricacy of God's Word, learning and exploring new ideas and concepts.

Will we boldly go where no man has gone before? Perhaps not, but let's enjoy our journey, digging out treasures, grasping biblical principles, and discovering mysteries revealed in God's Word and in God's time.

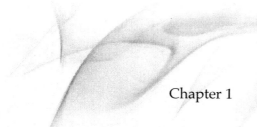

Chapter 1

THE DWELLING PLACE OF GOD

God has the ability to use one thing to teach many different things—from delicate shadings to colorful contrasts—all from the same events, elements or examples. Jesus taught in parables and stories. He would say one thing for the Pharisees to hear and later reveal deeper meanings to His disciples accompanied with phrases like: "Who hath ears to hear, let him hear" (Matthew 13:9).

A comprehensive study of the Old Testament Tabernacle in the wilderness would bring to light many valuable concepts we could apply in our lives.

- The Tabernacle has been used as an excellent model for prayer.
- The Tabernacle is a great tool to teach a step-by-step plan on how to separate from worldliness and sin and enter God's presence in purity.
- The Tabernacle reveals the seven annual feasts that correlate to aspects of our New Testament walks with God.

This is just a small sampling, and you may have come across something I haven't seen or considered. One thing most people who have studied the Tabernacle agree on is this: **The Tabernacle of Moses reveals the path for man to connect with God**—a path with the ultimate destination of spiritual intimacy with our Creator.

The Old Testament Tabernacle is an earthly creation of God's design. God was never limited to the Tabernacle. He is and has always been everywhere, but it was the connecting point between God and men. It revealed His plan to unite His holiness, truth and justness with His compassion, love and mercy for fallen mankind.

"Mercy and truth are met together; righteousness and peace have kissed each other" (Psalms 85:10).

What a beautiful picture the psalmist paints for us. This meeting—this kissing of mercy and truth—is exactly what happens in the Tabernacle, and the result is a sweet sensation. The terminology in this verse reveals a romantic God. And why shouldn't it? Who created the pleasure of a kiss or a touch in the first place? The Word of God says "Kiss the Son, lest he be angry" (Psalm 2:12). Note the word "Son" is capitalized, indicating a particular person, a certain heir—and this Son wants to be kissed.

Throughout our lives, as we walk with the Lord, our relationships with Him take on varying roles—Father-child; Master-servant; Friend-friend, Brother-sibling, etc. This study does not delve into these types of relationships, but explores what I believe is the ultimate desire of the Lord: intimacy in a Husband-wife relationship.

In addition to the Tabernacle, the Bible gives marriage as an earthly example to help us understand God's desire for spiritual intimacy with His people. Marriage between a man and a woman is given as an analogy of the relationship between Christ and the Church to the world (Ephesians 5:25-32). It is called a mystery, but that does not mean we should not explore the subject or try to understand its meaning.

A mystery is something that is hidden, but not necessarily to all. Although the marriage analogy is a concept not obviously understood, we can open the Word and our hearts, and God can bring understanding and revelation to us in the same way He opened the disciples' understanding to His teaching. "Unto you it is given to know the mysteries of the kingdom of God" (Luke 8:10).

There are mysteries in the Word, but look at what the Apostle Paul said. "I would not, brethren, that ye should be ignorant of this mystery" (Romans 11:25). In another epistle, he said the gospel is a mystery (Ephesians 6:19). It was previously hidden, but a mystery God now makes known to His saints (Colossians 1:26-27). That inspires me to prayerfully dig into the Word and see what the Lord will open to me—to you, His saints.

WHY EARTH?

Every element used to make the Tabernacle and its furnishings came from Earth, the same Earth God used to create the body of Adam and the physical body of Jesus Christ. Every fiber, every metal, every skin, every piece of wood used in the construction of the temple, its furnishings and implements, sprung up from the earth's waters and grounds (Genesis 1:12; 20; 24) or was buried within it.

One thing made me curious. Why did God choose the Earth over other planets? What attracted Him to the sphere we call home? "In the beginning God created the heaven and the earth" (Genesis 1:1). He filled the earth with His goodness (Psalm 33:5). **God made our planet with a special purpose in mind, and He has a notable attraction to it.**

- Satellite images of our world relay its compelling beauty. Earth is a blue planet, and it seems God has a thing for blue. Throughout Scripture He uses the color blue to symbolize His holiness.
- The earth's core is a said to reach 5,000 degrees Fahrenheit, hotter than any burning fire on its surface. "For the LORD thy God is a consuming fire, even a jealous God" (Deuteronomy 4:24). The Lord has a fiery attraction to His creation.
- Although we can't see it, the earth's interior is active. Our invisible God is active and working, too. "Behold, I go forward, but he is not there; and backward, but I cannot perceive him: On the left hand, where he doth work, but I cannot behold him: he hideth himself on the right hand, that I cannot see him" (Job 23:8-9).
- The earth generates a magnetic field, and most scientists believe our planet rotates around the sun. In traditional Jewish weddings it is customary for the bride to circle the groom seven times at the beginning of the ceremony as a symbol that, upon joining in marriage, her world will revolve around her husband.

SIDENOTE: Just to give your brain a jolt, there is a theory called geocentricity that claims the sun rotates around the earth. I am not a scientist and don't support the claim one way or the other, but Scripture does speak of an active sun, not an active planet. The sun rises (Genesis 19:23). It goes down (Genesis 15:12). It follows a circuit (Psalms 19:6). It miraculously stood still (Joshua 10:12).

The earth was created on the first day and the sun on the fourth (Genesis 1). The Lord said He compasses (circles) about His people, (Psalms 32:7) and the writer of Hebrews said we are compassed about by a great cloud of witnesses (Hebrews 12:1). "Of the heavens has God made a tent for the sun, Which is as a bridegroom coming out of his chamber" (Psalm 19:4-5).

GOD'S LONGING

Genesis doesn't give many details of the activities of Heaven before creation, but it does give cause for speculation. I've wondered if God felt betrayed, hurt or rejected after Satan rose up against Him. Did He miss Satan and the other angels that rebelled?

A study on Satan would fill another book. Without going too far off on another tangent so soon, the proper name Lucifer is mentioned only once in the Bible. Some speculate Lucifer and Satan are two different entities, but Jesus said He saw Satan cast down from heaven (Luke 10:17). Isaiah give's the name of the one cast down: Lucifer (Isaiah 14:12). In Ezekiel 28, although the prophet spoke to a historical person, the king of Tyrus, the text reveals that God sent Ezekiel to address the power behind the king—Satan, who was present in the Garden of Eden, an impossibility for a human king living in the 6th Century (Ezekiel 28:13).

I mention all this to make the point that God had been in relationship with Satan. Ezekiel 28 tells us this "anointed cherub that covereth" was beautiful. He was arrayed in gemstones that would have reflected the light of God's glory, but Satan became proud in his beauty and was corrupted. And in so doing, he lost out on true beauty—reflecting God's glory in purity and holiness. He lost out on the most important thing of all—a relationship with God.

Have you ever wondered if God and His loyal angels felt the void of lost relationship after Satan's rebellion? Heaven had empty places that hadn't been there before, and the Lord no longer had the pleasure of seeing His glory dance as it refracted off Lucifer's prisms in vibrant display.

Did God have a longing in His heart for someone who would choose to love Him and be faithful to Him just for Who He was and is? Is that why He created Adam and Eve? If my timeline is right, and Lucifer fell before Creation, it only makes sense that Satan was jealous over Adam. He wanted to drive a wedge between God and men, so he devised a plan. He persuaded Adam and Eve to ingest evil. He convinced them to take something God hated—disobedience and rebellion—and put it in something God loved—the bodies He had made for them. Satan is still using this same tactic today.

Thank God for His love. It was the love of God that sent a Redeemer to repair the breach of sin created by Adam and Eve's disobedience. Through Jesus' perfect obedience and sacrifice, restoration became available for all humanity—not the fallen angels who had already experienced heaven's perfection, but those who were weak, by God's own design, and accepted His redemption, His love and approval.

Chapter 2

SPIRITUAL INDWELLING PHYSICAL

The Tabernacle is the meeting place between God and men. In Rabbinic literature, called *Midrash*, the Tabernacle, also known as the Tent of Meeting, is compared to a cave near the sea. When the sea roars and floods the cave, the cave fills with water, but the sea isn't missing anything. In the same way, a manifestation of God's glorious *shekinah* presence filled the Tabernacle in the wilderness while His omnipresent Spirit simultaneously radiated over all the world.[1]

This analogy can also be applied to the Man, Christ Jesus, and the Spirit within Him—the Holy Spirit of our Father, the Creator, dwelling in the body of our Savior. The Holy Spirit filled the physical body of Jesus with His character, power and authority, all the while the Almighty God ruled and reigned over the universe. We will see this same concept in the Tabernacle of Moses and how it illustrates a lifestyle I call **"tabernacling with God"—an indwelling of the Spirit of the Lord, that leads and guides us, while at the same time we are covered and protected in a secret place with Him.**

Before we dive into our exploration of the anatomy of Moses' Tabernacle, let's take a brief look at the New Testament and what it has to say about tabernacles. Sometimes I just can't resist taking a peek in the back of the book. So we'll start with the ending, the book of Revelation, and the last tabernacle reference found in the Bible.

"And I John saw the holy city, new Jerusalem, coming down from God out of heaven, prepared as a bride adorned for her husband. And I heard a great voice out of heaven saying, Behold, the tabernacle of God is with men, and he will dwell with them, and they shall be his people, and God himself shall be with them, and be their God" (Revelation 21:2-3).

Strong's renders one of the translations for the word *city* in the above passage as "the abode of the blessed in heaven."[2] *New Jerusalem* means "the heavenly abode of God" as well as "a splendid visible city to be let down from heaven."[3] The word *tabernacle* refers to a physical tent made of skins and boughs or specifically Moses' Tabernacle.[4] And get this...the first meaning of the word translated *dwell* is "fix one's tabernacle, abide (or live) in a tabernacle."[5]

Let's read the passage with these expounded definitions in the unpublished and unauthorized "Lori Wagner Amplified Version:"

"And I John saw the holy 'abode of the blessed,' 'a splendid city let down from heaven,' prepared as a bride adorned for her husband. And I heard a great voice out of heaven saying, Behold, the 'tabernacle' (or) 'Tabernacle of Moses' is with men, and he will 'live in a tabernacle' with them, and they shall be his people, and God himself shall be with them, and be their God."

The real *Amplified Bible* (not the imaginary Lori Wagner version), translates the word *tabernacle* as "abode," while the *New International Version* calls it the "dwelling of God." The Tabernacle, from its conception in Exodus to its fulfilled purpose in Revelation, has always been the physical dwelling place for the Spirit of God.

This verse in Revelation reminds me of another. Flip back to Exodus.

"And they shall know that I am the LORD their God, that brought them forth out of the land of Egypt, that I may dwell among them: I am the LORD their God" (Exodus 29:46).

Dwelling with humanity seems to be God's original intention. Look back to the Garden of Eden and consider how God walked with Adam and Eve in the cool of each day. Before sin polluted the purity of their relationship, the Lord enjoyed His daily time with Adam and Eve, but disobedience created a dissatisfying breach between God and the people He loved.

Like the Garden planted by the Lord, the Tabernacle erected by Moses in the wilderness was the place God met His people. In

Revelation we read the Lord's promise that the Tabernacle of God will dwell among men. **Tabernacling, dwelling together in an enclosed and sacred place, has been in the heart of God from the beginning of time.**

Considering what we've examined in both the Old and New Testaments, a simple definition of a tabernacle could read: "a physical entity (something that has a real existence) that houses a spiritual entity (essential nature)." The Tabernacle of Moses was a physical structure that housed the Spirit of God. In the New Testament, we learn that human bodies are regarded as tabernacles (2 Peter 1:14; 2 Corinthians 5:1) and temples (2 Corinthians 6:16; 1 Corinthians 6:19). Our bodies are physical living structures that house spiritual beings.

RELATIONSHIP

The Israelites knew very little about God, but God knew all about them—their worries, hopes, anxieties, and fears. After the Lord delivered the people from Egyptian slavery, He used the time in the desert to reveal Himself to them. He showed them His power to save; His deliverance from oppression; His guidance in the desert; His provision for hunger and thirst; and so much more.

In the desert, the Israelites learned two of the most basic truths of God:

1. He wants to have relationship with people, and
2. Relationship comes on His terms.

Point two might sound harsh, but once we get a glimpse of God's character—His goodness and grace, we know humanity gets the better end of the deal. As the Israelite's grew in their relationships with God, they understood He was more than a sweet "Sugar Daddy" deliverer and provider. All aspects and attributes of God— His character, His nature, the essence of Who He is— affect human-God relationships. Here's an example: God is love, but He is also holy and requires holiness from His people. "I am the LORD who brought you up out of Egypt to be your God, therefore be holy, because I am holy" (Leviticus 11:45).

The various facets of God's nature reveal more of Who He is as a whole. One aspect of His personality does not negate others. Mercy does not nullify justice—quite the contrary. It was because of God's mercy He brought payment for justice's demands. Mercy and justice are both part of God's whole—like one plane or facet of a diamond reflecting a different quality or character of the stone. **Relationship with God is not a "smorgasbord" affair, where we pick and choose what we would like to fill our "God plates."** To have a relationship with God, we take Him as He is...and thank God He takes us as we are.

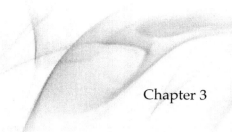

Chapter 3

ESTABLISHING COVENANT

We've peeked at the end of the Book, now let's go back to the beginning. The Tabernacle of Moses, the place where deity and humanity met, was about much more than a physical structure and furnishings. It represented the covenant between God and man—a covenant that began in the paradise of Eden and will be completed in the paradise of Heaven.

A covenant, or binding agreement, includes more than just legal aspects of an arrangement. **Covenant brings relationship.** It's a pledge or a promise. Covenant is a give-and-take alliance agreed upon by two or more parties.

The very first covenant, I believe, was established in the Garden of Eden. "And God blessed them, and God said unto them, Be fruitful, and multiply, and replenish the earth, and subdue it: and have dominion over the fish of the sea, and over the fowl of the air, and over every living thing that moveth upon the earth. And God said, Behold, I have given you every herb bearing seed, which is upon the face of all the earth, and every tree, in the which is the fruit of a tree yielding seed; to you it shall be for meat. And to every beast of the earth, and to every fowl of the air, and to every thing that creepeth upon the earth, wherein there is life, I have given every green herb for meat: and it was so" (Genesis 1:28-30).

"And the LORD God took the man, and put him into the garden of Eden to dress it and to keep it. And the LORD God commanded the man, saying, Of every tree of the garden thou mayest freely eat: But of the tree of the knowledge of good and evil, thou shalt not eat of it: for in the day that thou eatest thereof thou shalt surely die" (Genesis 2:15-17).

This covenant between Adam and Eve and God might not have the same generally accepted "label" or form as a typical biblical covenant, but look at its elements. It was an agreement initiated by God that included blessings of fruitfulness, promises for the coming generations, dominion, a beautiful land and an element of contingency. It came with responsibilities and a caveat; don't eat from the tree of the knowledge of good and evil. It was a give-and-take agreement between Adam and Eve and God.

Although their covenant was made in a perfect, sinless environment, Adam and Eve broke the terms of their agreement with God. This led me to think of the Genesis 3 encounter after the fall as an amendment to their original covenant. With His promise of a Messiah, God made a way to amend the death sentence Adam and Eve deserved as a result of breaking covenant.

Because of sin, God, in His mercy, made a provision for the people He loved. The amendment was sealed with the blood of the first animal sacrifice and God's promise to send a Messiah. If you take the time to read the details in Genesis 3, note the blood sacrifice, the covering of man by God and the presence of cherubim.

Centuries after the first covenant with Adam and Eve, God also established a covenant with Noah. This agreement parallels the one He made with Adam and Eve. It also included blessings of fruitfulness, promises for the coming generations, dominion, land and contingencies (Genesis 6:18; 9:13). Noah fulfilled the terms of the agreement when he built the ark and boarded it. When he and his family left the ark after the flood, Noah built an altar and offered sacrifices to the Lord. He received God's blessings of fruitfulness and a promise for the generations to come. This covenant was sealed with a rainbow.

God made a covenant with Abraham (Genesis 12:1-3), that passed to Isaac (Genesis 17:19), that passed to Jacob (Genesis 27), that passed to Joseph (Genesis 48:3-4), that passed to Ephraim (Genesis 5:1-2). **The covenants God made with each of these men in their generations**

were not new in their basic concepts, but re-establishments or renewals of the original covenant made with Adam and Eve.

But this book is about the Tabernacle, right? The Tabernacle Moses set up in the desert after the crossing of the Red Sea? Yes, it is. We will get there, but consider this: the Tabernacle was the means men used to meet with God according to the terms of their covenant with Him. God made a covenant with Moses and the Israelites at the time of the giving of the Law. Again, this wasn't really a new covenant, but a renewal of the covenant made with those who came before.

This covenant given to Moses on behalf of the people included blessings of fruitfulness, promises for the coming generations, dominion, land and a contingency that required obedience to the newly introduced ceremonial laws (Deuteronomy 28; Exodus 19-24). As in the Abrahamic Covenant, God also promised relationship, and as we will discover, communion with God in the Tabernacle, which included the presence of angels.

We don't know if God specifically revealed His plan of salvation in each of His covenant agreements, but we do know that each covenant was initiated by the Lord and men were the beneficiaries of God's outreach. God connected and contracted with men, and Jesus fulfilled the terms of the original covenant or testament. Through Jesus, relationship with God is now directly available to all.

A testament is an arrangement—a disposition of goods. We use the word "testament" in the phrase "last will and testament"—a legal document that signifies the author's request for dispersing his estate after his death. It also identifies the two segments of the Bible: the Old Testament and the New Testament. God's will, His testament, was fulfilled through the death of Jesus in the same way any person's will becomes valid—after the death of the one who made it.

"In the case of a will, it is necessary to prove the death of the one who made it, because a will is in force only when somebody has died; it never takes effect while the one who made it is living" (Hebrews 9:16-17, NIV).

The word translated "will" in the above passage is translated "testament" in *the King James Bible*. Let's look at the verses directly following these and see how this testament connects with the Tabernacle of Moses.

"This is why even the first covenant was not put into effect without blood. When Moses had proclaimed every commandment of the law to all the people, he took the blood of calves, together with water, scarlet wool and branches of hyssop, and sprinkled the scroll and all the people. He said, 'This is the blood of the covenant, which God has commanded you to keep.' In the same way, he sprinkled with the blood both the tabernacle and everything used in its ceremonies. In fact, the law requires that nearly everything be cleansed with blood, and without the shedding of blood there is no forgiveness.

"It was necessary, then, for the copies of the heavenly things to be purified with these sacrifices, but the heavenly things themselves with better sacrifices than these. For Christ did not enter a man-made sanctuary that was only a copy of the true one; he entered heaven itself, now to appear for us in God's presence" (Hebrews 9:18-24, NIV).

God revealed His redemption plan to Adam and Eve (Genesis 3:15). Scripture also tells us He shared His plan with Abraham.

"And the scripture, foreseeing that God would justify the heathen through faith, preached before the gospel unto Abraham, saying, In thee shall all nations be blessed" (Galatians 3:8). See also John 8:56.

The first covenant made in the Garden of Eden was the same covenant renewed and expanded over the generations. I compare it to a little girl passing different stages of growth until she is fully matured and ready to marry. She moved from birth, immaturity and selfishness to dignity, purpose and selflessness. There were setbacks as she grew—not due to God's lack of planning or His failed design, but because her free will consistently interloped in God's plans. Thank God Jesus came to perfect or complete the covenant.

The Tabernacle points to Jesus, Who through His execution, executed the terms of the testament or will made between God and men. Through His death, burial and resurrection, He fulfilled the commands that would usher in new life and relationship with God. With His blood He paid the price to redeem His creation, but like the original arrangement made in Eden, men and women are given the ability to choose or refuse the terms of the relationship.

Let me explain it better with this example: People list and sell houses all the time. It's a complicated process, and when closing day finally arrives everyone is usually happy. The papers are signed, the keys are passed, and new ownership is established. The purchasers, once the terms are complete, have every right to inhabit the home they just acquired, but until they cross town and turn the key in the lock, they haven't taken possession of what is rightfully theirs.

Resurrection Day was God's closing day. Jesus gave men the keys to eternal life, complete with housewarming gifts like knowledge, wisdom and discernment (Ephesians 4:8). It's up to us to put the key in the lock of our lives and take possession of our new homes in Him.

A PROPHETIC PICTURE

The Tabernacle of Moses has been called by many names:
- Tabernacle (tent or dwelling place)
- Sanctuary (Exodus 25:8)
- Tent of Meeting (Exodus 27:21)
- Tabernacle of Testimony (Exodus 38:21)
- The Temple of the Lord (1 Samuel 3:3)
- House of the Lord (Joshua 6:24)
- Tent of the Testimony (Numbers 9:15)
- Tent of the Congregation (Exodus 40:6)
- The Sacred Tent of Jehovah (*Strong's Concordance*)"[6]

Beyond its Old Testament function as the meeting place between men and God, the Tabernacle also provided a prophetic picture to the world. It was an earthly structure that revealed God's plan for men and women to restore the relationship broken by sin. The design of the Tabernacle is a straight path, an arrow that points directly from its Gate to the Holy of Holies where the Lord invites His bride to enter intimate, holy communion with Him.

I recently heard a teaching on the Tabernacle by Bishop G.A. Mangun. He said, "If we're going to get to Heaven, we need to get a little Heaven on Earth."[7] The Tabernacle of Moses is a bit of Heaven on Earth. Some things are already established in the spirit realm before we see them in our world. Remember Jesus' instructions to pray "on Earth as it is in Heaven" (Matthew 6:10).

God is a Spirit unconfined by finite parameters. He created the world in the beginning of time and declared the end from the beginning (Isaiah 46:10). As He gave the directions to Moses for the Tabernacle, He used His heavenly Tabernacle as its Master plan.

"Who serve unto the example and shadow of heavenly things, as Moses was admonished of God when he was about to make the tabernacle: for, See, saith he, that thou make all things according to the pattern shewed to thee in the mount" (Hebrews 8:5).

According to this verse, **the Tabernacle of Moses was an example, or copy—a shadow, an "express likeness"[8] of the true Tabernacle in Heaven**—a bit of Heaven on Earth. We can follow its clear directions to our destination, the ultimate Holy of Holies in Heaven. And this heavenly Tabernacle, the "true Tabernacle" was pitched by the Lord Himself, not men (Hebrews 8:2).

To make it to Heaven in the future, we follow the Tabernacle plan and prepare ourselves to enter into a holy place of communion with God in the here and now. You see, what we do on Earth will continue into eternity.

"He that is unjust, let him be unjust still: and he which is filthy, let him be filthy still: and he that is righteous, let him be righteous still: and he that is holy, let him be holy still" (Revelation 22:11).

Chapter 4

THE OUTER COURT

S o now, after all the stage-setting preamble, let's take a look at the anatomy and furnishings of the physical Tabernacle in the wilderness. Rather than spend a lot of time studying the specifications and details of the Tabernacle and its furnishings, we will take a cursory look at the major items to get an overview of their purpose, function and layout. We will examine the curtains and coverings and four furnishings: the Brazen Altar, the Brazen Laver, the Golden Candlestick and the Ark of the Covenant.

Looking from the outside in, the first thing we see of the Tabernacle is a perimeter fence enclosing a rectangular bit of ground approximately 150 feet long and 75 feet wide. This fence created a courtyard which might sometimes be confused with the Tabernacle itself. The Tabernacle proper, as you will see, does not include the fence, or even the altars within the fence. It is the name for the covered Holy Place in the interior of the courtyard.

"The length of the court shall be an hundred cubits, and the breadth fifty every where, and the height five cubits of fine twined linen, and their sockets of brass" (Exodus 27:18).

A finely woven yet unadorned linen fence created the Outer Court. It was a roofless structure always pitched in the same direction with a single entry situated in the center of the eastern wall.

THE GATE

"For the gate of the court there shall be a screen twenty cubits long, woven of blue, purple, and scarlet thread, and fine woven linen, made by a weaver. It shall have four pillars and four sockets" (Exodus 27:16).

The Tabernacle had one Gate. The orientation of the Gate was in direct contrast to the pattern used by pagan sun worshippers of the day. Israelites entered the Tabernacle to worship with the sun at their backs instead of facing and worshipping the rising sun.

Over the years I have often pictured God's people walking through the Gate into the Tabernacle's Court with praise, thanksgiving and blessings on their lips (see Psalm 100:4), but the Tabernacle of Moses, a solemn meeting place, had not yet experienced the type of worship David introduced during his reign as King. Although Miriam and Moses led quite a joyful worship service celebrating the crossing of the Red Sea and their deliverance from the Egyptians, no tambourines or dance or lively songs appeared to be included in worship in the first Tabernacle.

Forgive me for putting the cart before the horse, but as adopted members of God's family, descendants of the house of David, today's New Testament believers should follow the example set by David, our spiritual forefather, who taught us to begin our time with the Lord with thanksgiving and praise. This approach, rather than a formal, ceremonial one, gives a bit of insight into why so many people receive the infilling of the Holy Ghost when they begin praising God. **Praise is a gate that takes us from our physical world into the spiritual realm of God's presence.**

"But thou art holy, O thou that inhabitest the praises of Israel" (Psalm 22:3).

Further in our study we will examine how Solomon incorporated Davidic worship in the temple that eventually replaced the Tabernacle. There is a developing process of relationship and approach to God that builds and grows throughout Scripture. It's helpful for understanding to go back to the beginning and watch God unfold His plan from generation to generation, but remember, these concepts build on each other, precept upon precept, line upon line.

Keep in mind the Outer Court is not our ultimate destination. It is the first step on the path to the Holy of Holies, like the first step in a relationship where people meet and acknowledge one another. Meeting God at the Gate with praise, acknowledging Who He is— His might, His power, His goodness, His provision—this is just the beginning of a relationship God wants to take from "acquaintance" to "lover."

In contrast to the simple perimeter fence, the Gate, a screen-type entryway, featured vibrant colors rich with symbolism and meaning. Among other meanings, purple represented royalty, scarlet represented blood, white represented righteousness and blue indicated holiness. To those who entered the Tabernacle Gate, these colors served as reminders of several aspects of God's nature—aspects that led them and inspired them to give honor and sacrifice to a worthy God. As we enter our personal times with the Lord, the symbolism in these colors can expand our praise as we reflect on beautiful attributes of God and His character. There is much more to learn about the colors used in the Tabernacle and their symbolism. I will leave you to study that on your own as we stay on track to the Holy Place.

> SIDE NOTE: Some scholars propose the four posts of the Gate represent the four gospels: Matthew, Mark, Luke and John. I found no scriptural verification, but I thought I would include it for your consideration. If something we gloss over catches your interest, I encourage you to investigate and mine these treasures yourself. Studying the Word brings a rich reward.

Before we move on, take note of the absence of cherubim on the Tabernacle Gate or perimeter fence. As we draw near to God's presence, we'll see where God specifically instructed Moses to include cherubim in the Tabernacle's structure and furnishings. I hope you find it as exciting as I did.

THE BRAZEN ALTAR

"And thou shalt make an altar of shittim wood, five cubits long, and five cubits broad; the altar shall be foursquare: and the height thereof shall be three cubits. And thou shalt make the horns of it upon the four corners thereof: his horns shall be of the same: and thou shalt overlay it with brass. And thou shalt make his pans to receive his ashes, and his shovels, and his basons, and his fleshhooks, and his firepans: all the vessels thereof thou shalt make of brass. And thou shalt make for it a grate of network of brass; and upon the net shalt thou make four brasen rings in the four corners thereof. And thou shalt put it under the compass of the altar beneath, that the net may be even to the midst of the altar. And thou shalt make staves for the altar, staves of shittim wood, and overlay them with brass. And the staves shall be put into the rings, and the staves shall be upon the two sides of the altar, to bear it. Hollow with boards shalt thou make it: as it was shewed thee in the mount, so shall they make it" (Exodus 27:1-8).

The Outer Court housed two furnishings and their implements: the Brazen Altar and the Brazen Laver. The *King James* translation of the Bible records these items were made of brass; however, brass, as we know it today is an alloy of copper and zinc that was not developed until the 13th Century. The Hebrew word *nĕchosheth*, translated brass in the Bible, refers to a hardened or tempered copper.[9]

It's not necessary for our purposes to go into all the dimensions and details of the Brazen Altar, also known as the Altar of Sacrifice, or literally "slaughter place." Just know this was the busiest place in the temple and the first furnishing inside the Gate. It was a large square structure with a ramp leading up to it—a place where animals and birds were slain and roasted, fruits of the ground were offered and where blood and coals were collected.

The Brazen Altar, with its fires continually burning, was the place of repentance. It was here sacrifice offerings were routinely burned every morning and evening and where sin and fellowship offerings were presented to the Lord. One thing you might not be aware of—something I found interesting—was the person bringing an animal to be sacrificed as an offering for sin was the same person responsible for killing it. I used to assume the priests killed the animals given for sacrifice, but not so in the case of sin. After the animal or bird was slaughtered, the priests prepared it and placed it on the fire, but the one bringing a sin offering was the one responsible for killing it (Leviticus 4:24). If, as in days of old, I had to personally kill the animal whose innocent blood would cover my sin, perhaps I would consider more carefully the weight and consequences of my actions.

Through Jesus' sacrifice on the altar of the cross, our ultimate Passover Lamb (John 1:29), we no longer have to make blood sacrifices to atone for our sins (Hebrews 7:27). When He gave His life, He said, "It is finished," signifying the debt for sin had been paid and the need for animal sacrifices ended.

Yes, the price has been paid, but until we are "like Him" (1 John 3:2), we will continue to deal with flesh and sin. With this in mind, Christians today must continue to maintain an altar of repentance in our lives—a place where we burn off sin—unintentional transgressions and willful violations of God's Word in our behavior, conduct and attitudes. We must examine our hearts and take a careful inspection to see if pride or rebellion have taken root there. These very fertile, inordinately self-focused attitudes resist the things of God and can ultimately grow into consuming sin.

To maintain our walks with God and grow in our relationships with Jesus, we need to regularly visit a place where we incinerate anything that is not Christ-like and become living sacrifices for Him (Romans 12:1). In the New Testament, the Apostle Paul said, "I die daily" (1 Corinthians 15:21). In the Old Testament example of the Tabernacle, daily sacrifices were made at the Brazen Altar every morning and evening.

THE BRAZEN LAVER

"Thou shalt also make a laver of brass, and his foot also of brass, to wash withal: and thou shalt put it between the tabernacle of the congregation and the altar, and thou shalt put water therein. For Aaron and his sons shall wash their hands and their feet thereat: When they go into the tabernacle of the congregation, they shall wash with water, that they die not; or when they come near to the altar to minister, to burn offering made by fire unto the LORD" (Exodus 30:18-20).

The Brazen Laver was situated in a straight line between the Brazen Altar and the tent called the Tabernacle or the Holy Place. The metal basin, also fashioned of hardened or tempered copper, was made from material acquired by a unique source—the copper mirrors of Jewish women who donated them for use in the Tabernacle. The Laver had no set dimensions, and every mirror donated was used in its construction.

Moses objected to the use of these mirrors. He considered them inappropriate for God's sacred meeting place. Hebrew wives had previously used them during the centuries of enslavement in Egypt to entice their exhausted husbands to romantic relationships. Moses did not want to make a sacred object out of materials used to incite sexual relations, but God intervened and gave His approval of these mirrors that had been used to preserve His lineage through marital intimacy. With His approval He sent a message to Moses and those of us looking on the Tabernacle today, that holiness and sexuality between husband and wife are not contradictory one to another, a message affirmed in the New Testament. "Marriage is honourable in all" (Hebrews 13:4a).

Priests primarily used the Laver to wash after offering sacrifices—not just a ceremonial water ritual, but an actual cleansing of their hands and feet of the ashes and blood of the sacrifices. The priests washed at (not in) the Laver, an act that correlates to the washing of the Word in the New Testament (Ephesians 5:26). Scripture parallels this "washing of the Word" with the husband-wife relationship and the Christ-Church relationship.

"Husbands, love your wives, even as Christ also loved the church, and gave himself for it; That he might sanctify and cleanse it with the washing of water by the word, That he might present it to himself a glorious church, not having spot, or wrinkle, or any such thing; but that it should be holy and without blemish" (Ephesians 5:25-27).

The activity at the Brazen Laver, beyond Old Testament protocol, is a key component in a New Testament believer's walk with God. **Daily cleansing follows daily sacrifice**—a good model to follow. Clean hands are hands ready to serve. Clean feet are feet that walk in integrity before God and men. Looking into the Bible, our personal "brazen lavers," we see reflections of the impurities in our lives that need cleansing by the Word of God. As we read it, our minds and spirits are washed and restored.

In addition to physical cleansing, the Laver was also used to reestablish trust between husbands and wives (Numbers 5:11-31). When a husband felt jealous or concerned that his wife had been unfaithful, but he had no evidence to prove it, the couple appeared before the priest at the Brazen Laver. The directions outlined in Numbers 5 made it possible for the husband and wife to renew their trust and restore their relationship.

As the Bride of Christ, we often give the Lord reason for jealousy. It is at the Brazen Laver of cleansing we are able to restore broken trust or infidelity with our heavenly Bridegroom.

SIDE NOTE: Before the priest performed this ritual between a husband and wife and before the Lord, he uncovered the woman's hair. *Para`*, the Hebrew word for "uncover" used in Numbers 5:18, is also rendered "to make naked" (from the idea of loosening, casting off the garments), e.g. the head."[10]

The Laver made with the mirrors used previously in Jewish bedchambers was the place of physical cleansing. It was a washing that represented spiritual cleansing. The Laver was the place where husbands and wives restored marital relationships and priests prepared themselves to enter the Holy Place of intimacy with God.

The Outer Court, with its Brazen Altar and Laver, represents the first level of intimacy with God. It is here God is recognized and flesh is slaughtered. It is in the Outer Court we acknowledge sin, ask for forgiveness, give sacrifices and offerings, and set shaky marital relationships aright.

In the Outer Court, the main focus of the priests was serving and ministering to and on behalf of the people. The majority of the Israelites were not allowed beyond this point, but in the new covenant, God's people fulfill the role of "royal priesthood" (1 Peter 2:9), "holy priesthood" (1 Peter 2:5), and have access to the Tabernacle's most sacred and holy chamber.

The Outer Court was a messy, tiresome and emotional area, but a place where people found healing, forgiveness and restoration. Good things happened in the Outer Court, **but we are not meant to stay locked into "Outer Court relationship,"** focused primarily on praise and repentance, offerings and cleansing. It's easy to get sidetracked here with all the commotion and activities going on— focused on the personal needs of ourselves and others—and not enter into the relationship we have access to in the inner parts of the Tabernacle. Remember, the Outer Court is only the beginning of our walks with God. It may be tempting to let our Outer Court experiences deter us from God's ultimate plan for intimacy, but we are on a journey to the Holy Place.

Repentance is not enough. Cleansing is not enough. Sacrifices and offerings are not enough. The things done in the Outer Court were done in preparation to enter the Holy of Holies.

Chapter 5

THE TABERNACLE

After completing his Outer Court preparations, the priest was ready to enter the Tabernacle, a tent also called the Holy Place. In the Holy Place attention turned from ministering to and on behalf of man, to interacting personally with God.

If you're with me up to this point, this is where you might decide to write me off as a fruit loop—or maybe you'll jump in the cereal box with me. Many consider the Tabernacle a portrait of Jesus. When I began to study and reflect on the Tabernacle, I considered the entire Tabernacle area, from its core to its perimeter fence, a representation of the physical body of Jesus. Further digging led me to a different conclusion.

I've come to consider the Tabernacle area at large as a physical representation of the dwelling place for the Spirit of Almighty God. Of course, God is a Spirit and has no "perimeter fence," but He used the Tabernacle to reveal Himself to men...more than perhaps they understood at the time.

Within the Tabernacle courtyard, meticulously covered and prepared as a bridal chamber, the Israelites raised the tent called the Holy Place with its inner compartment, the Most Holy Place or Holy of Holies. This is the seat of intimacy, and as we will see, a foretelling of the coming relationship Christ will have with His betrothed. **Not yet revealed to the Israelites of old, the inner chamber of the Holy of Holies serves as a representation of God in flesh, Jesus,** our Messiah and King, the promise made in the Garden of Eden and confirmed through the ages by His prophets.

Think for a moment with me how the anatomy of the Tabernacle lays out and relates to the anatomy of a human body. As we've already discussed, there is an "on-Earth-as-it-is-in-Heaven" concept surrounding the Tabernacle. It is a physical picture of a spiritual concept that surpasses the limitations of time and carnal understanding—a plan that brings God's Bride into His chamber. Through Scripture we catch beautiful glimpses as the light of God's Spirit shines on His Word, but the magnificence and awe and majesty of God's plan are more than we can truly comprehend, much less transmit with words. The Apostle Paul said he could not even speak of the things he once saw in a spiritual vision (2 Corinthians 12:4).

If we can't really understand, then why bother studying or discussing the subject of the Tabernacle? That's a good question. The answer is that we *can* see—but in part, as through a dark glass (1 Corinthians 13:12). It's like the tinted windows in the back of my minivan. A quick glance from far away doesn't reveal what's inside, but if you get up close and focus, you can see a lot more detail.

In the Word, we see the symbolism shadows that speak of what lies ahead without grasping the intricate details and magnitude of God's plan (Hebrews 10:1). Speaking specifically about the Tabernacle, the writer of Hebrews said the priests "serve unto the example and shadow of heavenly things, as Moses was admonished of God when he was about to make the tabernacle: for, See, saith he, that thou make all things according to the pattern shewed to thee in the mount (Hebrews 8:5).

God gave Moses the Tabernacle as a shadow of heavenly things and, oh, the glory to come. I'm excited for that day! For now, let's take a look and see what we can discover that will enrich our walks with God in the here and now. Just look at this:

"For ye are dead, and your life is hid with Christ in God" (Colossians 3:3). Think about the order, the "layout" of this verse and how it relates to our relationship with God. **Our lives are hidden *with* Jesus—where?** *In* **God.** We are hidden, we are covered with Jesus in God. I know I repeated that, but it's worth repeating, isn't it?

Look now at the Tabernacle. Imagine its perimeter as a fine white linen robe worn by our unseen God. We greet Him with kisses of praise at the mouth of the skeletal Tabernacle structure covered in linen.

Is it kosher to think of God wearing white linen? After all, He's a spiritual being. Does He need clothes anyway? Revelation 15:6 tells of angels clothed in pure, white linen. Angels are spiritual beings. Do they need clothing? Revelation 18:16 says the city called Babylon was clothed in linen. A city clothed in fabric? Could this be literal, or is it a metaphor? Of course, God is bigger than the Tabernacle and His magnitude cannot be encompassed solely in the parameters of a linen fence. It's like the ocean/cave analogy we discussed before. God was and is everywhere, but He sets certain meeting places and occasions to connect directly with men.

God seems to have a preference for clean white linen. The Levitical priesthood wore white linen as they ministered in the Tabernacle (2 Chronicles 5:12). God's heavenly armies will come robed in white linen (Revelation 19:14), and His wife will also wear white linen (Revelation 19:7-8).

Let's take a peek beneath the fabric and see what we will find. Please keep in mind that I don't claim this interpretation is the only way to view the Tabernacle, but one of many beautiful pictures of God that reveals His desire for intimacy with men.

The Brazen Altar, the place of repentance and sacrifice, is a likely representation of the heart of God. According to Dr. David Norris, author of *I Am*, an extensive study on the nature and names of God, the primary characteristic of God revealed in the Old Testament was His holiness, followed by His justice.[11] Before the birth of Jesus, more than any other aspects of His nature, God's holiness and justness held center stage. "Holy" is Who and What God is, and His justness is a key factor in His relationship with men and angels.

Other facets of God's nature—His divinity, lordship, love, goodness, purity and more—bring further revelation of His nature—all adding to and not detracting from His core essence.

It is because of His holy and just nature God required atonement and sacrifice for sin on the Brazen Altar before anyone could enter further into relationship with Him. Holiness and justness are at the core of the essence of God. The Brazen Altar was a place created as a result of God's love.

The next item, **the Brazen Laver, represents the seat of emotions and affections which correlates in Scripture with the physical organ of the reins (kidneys)** located below the heart in the abdomen. *Strong's* translates *reins* as the "inmost mind" and "inmost soul,"[12] and we often find reins and heart joined together in the Word (Psalm 7:9; 26:2; Jeremiah 11:20; Revelation 2:22).

In direct correlation with the role of washing at the Brazen Laver, the primary function of kidneys is to remove waste from the body. Priests removed the residue—the blood and ashes of the sacrifices—at the copper basin, what I propose as a typology of the "reins" of the Lord. Without reins to filter and eliminate impurities in our bodies, there is no life in the body. Dialysis, an outward intervention from another source, may sustain life for some time, but a healthy body requires healthy reins—purified minds, souls and emotions.

THE HOLY PLACE

Within the fenced courtyard, beyond the Brazen Altar and Brazen Laver, the priests erected the Tabernacle. This tent-like structure, also called the Holy Place, had four distinct coverings. It was a protected, sacred compartment divided into two distinct sections by a veil.

God covers and protects the things He cares for—those things He sets apart for Himself. He hides from public view the holy and sacred. I prayerfully present this abstract to you—not to indicate the Holy Place of the Tabernacle was a place of literal reproductive parts—but that it represents a spiritual union exemplified in physical interplay. The Holy Place was the place humanity and deity met. Physical interaction between the priest and Ark of the Covenant occurred in this holy chamber, but the natural affairs represented deeper spiritual happenings.

At the time of the Tabernacle of Moses, God did not yet inhabit the physical body of Jesus on Earth, but remember, the Tabernacle was a shadow of what already existed in Heaven—a place outside time's boundaries where God and mankind will unite in Heaven's Holy of Holies. There was a lot of symbolism in the Tabernacle illustration—a spiritual picture that reveals:

1) covering,
2) intimacy, and
3) sacredness are part of an intertwining relationship.

In the book *Roman Honor* by Carlin Barton, the author explains how the Latin word *verenda,* which means "parts of the body to be regarded with awe or reverence," intertwines with the word *pudenda,* which refers to "parts to be protected by shame."[13] The Romans believed private reproductive parts should be regarded with awe or reverence and also protected. Body parts were not considered "shameful" because of their appearance or function, but only when they were violated, which could be accomplished by something as simple as staring or spoken words.

Barton cited social psychologist Kurt Riezler who said "*Pudenda* (the parts to be protected) and *veneranda* (parts to be regarded with awe or reverence) imply each other.[14] They indicate or suggest one another without being directly related.

So what is the point of including this information on a study of the Tabernacle? Consider with me that the intimate, sacred, holy parts of the Tabernacle were covered by tents and curtains. They were concealed from public view, protected, revered and awed. So allow me to reiterate that God covers and protects holy and sacred things—from human bodies to spiritual intimacy. What could be more holy or sacred or pure than intimacy with God?

Before going any further, let's take a look at the concept of Christ and the Church. I'm not attempting to shock anyone, truly, but think about the things already preached and discussed in churches everywhere—common understanding and teaching on marital intimacy between a husband and wife. We know what the Bible is talking about when it refers to a man and woman becoming one flesh. We also know the marriage relationship between a man and a woman is an example of the relationship between Jesus and His bride, the Church. Jesus is looking for marital intimacy, but in our modesty or discretion, we are afraid to look at "intimacy" with God in the same context as the example He gave us—spouses "knowing" one another.

Of course, intimacy has many facets. Physical intimacy is only one part of a marital union that in no way encompasses all the deep and significant aspects of relationship. It is, however, a central part of marriage—a physical act that consummates covenant vows.

HOLY PLACE COVERINGS

Let's look at the Tabernacle's **four distinct coverings**. Exposed to the sun, wind and rain, the outermost covering of the Tabernacle was made of what the *King James Bible* calls badger skins. The Hebrew *tachash,* translated "badger,"[15] is an obscure word used in the Bible exclusively for the temple coverings (Exodus 26) and once in reference to shoes (Ezekiel 16:10). Biblical scholars propose the term refers to a form of marine life. The *International Standard Bible Encyclopedia* indicates the animals were seals, sea cows, porpoises or dugongs, leaning more heavily to the dugongs that grazed along the shores of the Red Sea.

Dugongs are mammals born with thick creamy skin that darkens to brownish to dark gray over time. Their barrel-shaped bodies are sparsely covered in short hair, and they can get quite large—over 600 pounds. Their hides have been confirmed in the making of shoes worn by Arabs in Sinai,[16] and these skins would have provided a fairly waterproof outer covering for the Tabernacle.

I couldn't help noticing the dugong's skin's resemblance to human flesh. God created a body for Himself in Jesus. This body was the dwelling place of God in the earth—the meeting place between men and God. Spiritual and physical merged within the body of Jesus, and it is through this body God touched humanity in a flesh-to-flesh meeting.

Beneath the outermost skin covering was another layer of protection: a rams' skin covering dyed red. Are you getting the same picture I did? The anatomical similarities between the outermost flesh-colored skin, directly over a blood-red layer, looks to me like a picture of a human body. Beneath our skin, red blood circulates throughout our bodies.

The next layer, one step closer to the inner sanctuary of the Holy Place, is a covering made of curtains of goats' hair (Exodus 26:7). Scripture compares human hair to goats' hair (1 Samuel 19:13; Song 4:1). Particularly in the Song of Solomon, long flowing hair, like a flock of goats on a mountain (like a curtain, perhaps), attracted the lover to intimacy. So we see skin, blood and hair. What's next?

Beneath the goats' hair was a final covering made of fine linen. This is the covering the priests would see as they ministered inside the Holy Place. Blue, scarlet and purple, the same colors used on the Tabernacle Gate, were worked into the linen (Exodus 26:1-6). Cherubim embroidered in these curtains seemed to float in the inner chamber of the Tabernacle. Since this covering was on the top and sides, cherubim surrounded the priests in the Holy Place— above, around and behind as they ministered to the Lord. The inner curtains give a picture of the heavenly throne room where angels minister before the Lord.

Remember, cherubim have been in the presence of God since before the Garden. They were with Him in Heaven, and it was the Lord's specific instructions that images of them be woven into the curtains of the innermost chamber of the Holy Place. The Tabernacle is a beautiful picture of Heaven and perfect communion with God, which includes the presence of angels beneath a holy, sacred covering, a picture of Heaven on Earth.

THE DOOR

Before he entered the Holy Place, the priest first passed through a Door. This curtain created and embroidered with the same colors as the Tabernacle Gate, was not used by the general population of Israel. The masses were instructed to enter the Tabernacle through the Gate—the "straight gate" that led to a direct path to the Door of the Holy Place. Only a select few were allowed to enter the Door.

I find it significant that **Jesus called Himself the Door** (see John 10:9), not the Gate. It is through the Door of the Holy Place we enter into fellowship and intimacy with our Savior—not simply the Gate of Outer Court relationship.

THE GOLDEN CANDLESTICK

The first room of the Tabernacle, the Holy Place, housed three pieces of furniture: the Golden Candlestick, the Altar of Incense and the Table of Shewbread.

In contrast to the tempered copper furnishings of the Outer Court, the Tabernacle's furnishings were made of pure gold or of wood covered in pure gold.

"And thou shalt make a candlestick of pure gold: of beaten work shall the candlestick be made: his shaft, and his branches, his bowls, his knops, and his flowers, shall be of the same" (Exodus 25:31).

The first furnishing, the Golden Candlestick, or Golden Lampstand, stood to the left of the Door and was the only source of light inside the Holy Place. Made by anointed and skilled artisans of one solid piece of gold, the intricate and beautiful Candlestick weighed around 100 pounds.

Only ritually pure priests were authorized to tend the Candlestick. Twice daily, every morning and night, those appointed to serve in the Tabernacle checked its wicks and filled it with pure beaten olive oil (Exodus 27:20). The light from the Candlestick, which represented the Spirit of God, illuminated the other furnishings in the Holy Place, and **the glow from the Candlestick allowed the attending priest to fulfill**

his ministry before the Lord. In the same way, God's Spirit shining in our lives enables us to fulfill our call to minister to those in our world.

In the New Jerusalem to come, Jesus' light alone will illuminate the great city (Revelation 21:23-24). Until that day, every day, like the high priests of old, we must ensure the fire of the Holy Ghost burns brightly in our lives. We must tend our wicks and fill our vessels with oil every morning and night so the light of God illuminates our path. Otherwise, we may stumble and lose our way before we reach our ultimate destination—the Most Holy Place.

THE TABLE OF SHEWBREAD

"Thou shalt also make a table of shittim wood...overlay it with pure gold, and make thereto a crown of gold round about...And thou shalt make the dishes thereof, and spoons thereof, and covers thereof, and bowls thereof, to cover withal: of pure gold shalt thou make them. And thou shalt set upon the table shewbread before me alway" (Exodus 25:23-24; 29-30).

The Table of Shewbread, to the right of the Tabernacle Door, was a place to simply show bread—to lay it out before the Lord. Twelve loaves, historically considered unleavened, represented the twelve tribes of Israel and were set out in two neat stacks. Each stack of six was topped with a golden cup used to hold frankincense, and every week, before the Sabbath began on Friday evening, several priests ceremoniously carried fresh bread in prior to the removal of the old. The bread from the previous week was taken to a holy place and eaten by ritually clean priests. The frankincense was burned before the Lord (Leviticus 24:1-8).[17]

Called appropriately the "bread of presence," **Shewbread remained continually before the Lord indicating perpetual relationship and fellowship between God and His people.** The bread was a physical representation of the promises of God that His priests ingested. The Table of Shewbread was a place of continual connection between the Lord and His priests as they shared the holy bread in sacred covenant meals.

It would be hard to miss the parallel between the Table of Shewbread and the Lord's Supper. But it's a parallel with a twist, if you will. The Israelites kept loaves of bread before the Lord as a memorial of their twelve tribes, while Jesus asked His followers to observe communion in His memory (1 Corinthians 11:24-25).

When the priests ate the bread offered before the Lord, it created unity—a oneness between them, the Lord, and the people they represented. As they digested it, the bread became a part of them. Jesus called Himself the Bread of Life (John 6:35). Through the offering of His body, broken for all, we His people gain more than physical sustenance. We obtain spiritual nourishment through fellowship and communion with Him. We unite with Him as we share the Lord's Supper, a sacred covenant meal that brings us into oneness with God and our brothers and sisters in Christ.

THE ALTAR OF INCENSE

"And thou shalt make an altar to burn incense upon: of shittim wood shalt thou make it. A cubit shall be the length thereof, and a cubit the breadth thereof; foursquare shall it be: ...And thou shalt overlay it with pure gold...And two golden rings shalt thou make to it under the crown of it, by the two corners thereof, upon the two sides of it shalt thou make it; and they shall be for places for the staves to bear it withal" (Exodus 30:1-4).

Positioned between the Golden Candlestick and Table of Shewbread, but deeper inside the Tabernacle, the Altar of Incense stood in front of the Veil that separated the Holy Place from the Most Holy Place. This Altar's box-like shape was made of wood covered in gold.

SIDE NOTE: As I was studying this unique piece of furniture, I noticed it was the only Tabernacle furnishing made with two hooks (instead of four) on its corners (literally "ribs") and carried by poles that would in all probability be removed after the Altar was set in place. It doesn't seem logical a pole could rest securely in one hook, and Scripture does not specify where the Altar's poles were kept as it does with other Tabernacle furnishings. The Brazen Altar, Table of Shewbread and Ark of the Covenant each had four hooks, and the poles used to transport them were kept within the hooks at all times.

We may never know why the Altar of Incense was made with only two hooks. Perhaps it was simply smaller, but I think it's good to ponder, question and expand our minds as we study the Word and discover some of the mysteries and treasures it contains.

It was at the Altar of Incense that a mixture of spices, frankincense and salt was poured out on hot coals. This incense released a pleasing fragrance in the Holy Place. It is crucial to note the coals used to burn incense before the Lord were delivered by the priests *exclusively* from the Brazen Altar of Sacrifice. Aaron's sons, Tabernacle priests Nadab and Abihu, lost their lives when they ignored this instruction from God and used fire from a different "strange" source (Leviticus 10:1-2). The lesson here, I believe, is **that repentance absolutely must be made prior to ministering before the Lord**—something as a worship leader I try to always keep in mind before stepping on the platform.

Priests mediated for the people at the Altar of Incense which was continually lit before the presence of the Lord in the Most Holy Place. Every morning and evening they made regular offerings, and on the Day of Atonement, the high priest sprinkled blood on the Altar's horns before he took off his priestly outer robes and entered the Most Holy Place.

It seems to me God is into smells. He likes the fragrance of roasted grain, lamb, steaks and fowl, as well as perfumes and incense. Think about this: you and I, New Testament believers, are called the very aroma of Christ.

"For we are to God the aroma of Christ among those who are being saved and those who are perishing." (2 Corinthians 2:15, NIV).

Nothing is sweeter than the smell of your own baby, and the Lord says we are like the fragrance of His Son. The Bible calls our prayers incense, and they are mixed with incense offered before the Lord.

"Let my prayer be set forth before thee as incense" (Psalm 141:2a).

"And the smoke of the incense (the perfume) arose in the presence of God, with the prayers of the people of God (the saints), from the hand of the angel" (Revelation 8:4, AMP).

Why are these verses important? Because in them we see a continuation of the "on-Earth-as-it-is-in-Heaven" pattern. In Heaven there are both altar and incense, and as we discussed previously, in the Tabernacle, the Lord provided an example on terra firma that shows us the way to our heavenly home.

It was at the Altar of Incense an angel of the Lord appeared to a priest named Zechariah. He gave him joyful news—his barren wife would have a child—a child who became known as John the Baptist. I don't believe it is a coincidence Zechariah's son declared to his world the Tabernacle's message to humanity:

"He said, I am the voice of one crying in the wilderness, Make straight the way of the Lord" (John 1:23a).

The pattern of the Tabernacle in the wilderness was a straight path to the Lord. If we look at its layout—from the straight line of the Outer Court's Altar and Laver, to the arrangement of the inner furnishings, we see **a physical arrow pointing to the innermost chamber—the Most Holy Place.**

"And the LORD said unto Moses, Take unto thee sweet spices, stacte, and onycha, and galbanum; these sweet spices with pure frankincense: of each shall there be a like weight: And thou shalt make it a perfume, a confection after the art of the apothecary, tempered together, pure and holy" (Exodus 30:34).

The incense Zechariah offered before the Lord was made of stacte and onycha. Stacte, according to the *International Standard Bible Encyclopedia*, comes from two sources: one is pure myrrh.[18] *Gesenius's Lexicon* notes that onycha comes from a muscle found in the lakes of India that gives off a scent similar to musk.[19] Galbanum is a strong-smelling gum that preserved the musky, pungent scent poured out on the coals of the Altar of Incense.[20]

Think about that: frankincense and myrrh from the Table of Shewbread and the Tabernacle's incense were both poured out on a golden altar. Where have we read about gold, frankincense and myrrh before?

THE VEIL

"And thou shalt make a vail of blue, and purple, and scarlet, and fine twined linen of cunning work: with cherubims shall it be made: And thou shalt hang it upon four pillars of shittim wood overlaid with gold: their hooks shall be of gold, upon the four sockets of silver. And thou shalt hang up the vail under the taches, that thou mayest bring in thither within the vail the ark of the testimony: and the vail shall divide unto you between the holy place and the most holy" (Exodus 26:31-33).

The Veil, a beautiful curtain, separated the two sections of the Tabernacle: the Holy Place and the Most Holy Place, also called the Holy of Holies. Made of the same design as the curtains of the innermost part of the Tabernacle, the Veil separated men from personal interaction with God. Note again the presence of cherubim, the guardians of God's glory.

Chapter 6

THE HOLY OF HOLIES

The configuration of the Tabernacle and its Outer Court is similar to Bedouin tents still in use today. Depending on a person's wealth, tent dwellers own(ed) few or several poles used to subdivide larger tents into rooms. Though I found no biblical reference, I've read that Abraham and Sarah lived in such a three-room tent made of an entry, a guest area and a private bed chamber.

You can see the parallel to the Tabernacle layout, with its Outer Court entry, Holy Place guest area and private Holy of Holies. **The chamber of the Holy of Holies is the place of intimacy**, the bedroom, if you will—while at the same time, the throne room of God. How can that be? Because God is both Lover and King.

The Holy of Holies is the place the Almighty God spiritually unites with ordinary men. This reminds me of Esther. A common Hebrew girl, Esther was not of royal lineage or worthy according to worldly standards to be queen, but she was chosen by King Xerxes. When she, a common person, was drawn into the inner chamber, she became royalty through intimacy with the king. The same transformation will occur when Jesus takes His bride.

THE ARK OF THE COVENANT

Let's take a look at the furnishings in the Holy of Holies—or should I say furnishing? Only one item stood in the inner sanctum of the Most Holy Place—the Ark of the Covenant.

"And they shall make an ark of shittim wood: two cubits and a half shall be the length thereof, and a cubit and a half the breadth thereof, and a cubit and a half the height thereof. And thou shalt overlay it with pure gold, within and without shalt thou overlay it, and shalt make upon it a crown of gold round about. And thou shalt cast four rings of gold for it, and put them in the four corners thereof; and two rings shall be in the one side of it, and two rings in the other side of it. And thou shalt make staves of shittim wood, and overlay them with gold. And thou shalt put the staves into the rings by the sides of the ark, that the ark may be borne with them. The staves shall be in the rings of the ark: they shall not be taken from it. And thou shalt put into the ark the testimony which I shall give thee.

"And thou shalt make a mercy seat of pure gold: two cubits and a half shall be the length thereof, and a cubit and a half the breadth thereof. And thou shalt make two cherubims of gold, of beaten work shalt thou make them, in the two ends of the mercy seat. And make one cherub on the one end, and the other cherub on the other end: even of the mercy seat shall ye make the cherubims on the two ends thereof. And the cherubims shall stretch forth their wings on high, covering the mercy seat with their wings, and their faces shall look one to another; toward the mercy seat shall the faces of the cherubims be. And thou shalt put the mercy seat above upon the ark; and in the ark thou shalt put the testimony that I shall give thee. And there I will meet with thee, and I will commune with thee from above the mercy seat, from between the two cherubims which are upon the ark of the testimony, of all things which I will give thee in commandment unto the children of Israel" (Exodus 25:10-22).

The beautiful golden Ark of the Covenant, covered with the wings of golden cherubim, was the only object in the Holy of Holies, the inner chamber and throne room of the Tabernacle of God's presence among men. Before the high priest entered on his once-a-year visit, he completed his preparations in the Holy Place at the Altar of Incense, then discarded his priestly outer garments ornamented with embroidered pomegranates, tinkling bells, stones and precious gems. To enter the Holy of Holies, he wore no outer adornment that called attention to himself or his role as high priest. Instead, when he walked behind the Veil and offered blood on the Mercy Seat, he wore a simple white robe.

What the priest did annually, Jesus did once and for all. He came as both Lamb and High Priest.

"But [that appointed time came] when Christ (the Messiah) appeared as a High Priest of the better things that have come and are to come. [Then] through the greater and more perfect tabernacle not made with [human] hands, that is, not a part of this material creation, He went once for all into the [Holy of] Holies [of heaven], not by virtue of the blood of goats and calves [by which to make reconciliation between God and man], but His own blood, having found and secured a complete redemption (an everlasting release for us)" (Hebrews 9:11-12, AMP).

Remember the earthly Tabernacle is a shadow of what already exists in Heaven. Jesus offered His own blood in Heaven's Holy of Holies—a giving of Himself that ripped the Veil separating men from God in the earthly Holy Place.

True worship—pure, adoring reverence for God should result in giving ourselves completely to Him—holding nothing back. **Sincere devotion includes trust and allows entry into our innermost selves without restrictions or barriers or safety zones.** Figuratively we strip away the trappings of our world symbolized by the priest's ceremonial dress, and don the pure white linen covering the Lord has provided for us. Jesus paid a great price that we might enter behind the Veil to worship in the joy of restored relationship. We bask, sin-free in His presence, just as Adam and Eve experienced unadulterated communion with God in the Garden of Eden.

In the Most Holy Place of the Tabernacle, surrounded by cherubim, God showed up in a cloud of glory (Exodus 40:34). *Kabad,* the root of the word translated "glory," is associated with honor and also heaviness.[21] In the inner chamber of the Most Holy Place, we receive the weight of God's glory bearing down on us in a personal, intimate connection. I hope I'm expressing my thoughts well enough that you understand I am not talking about a physical meeting, but a spiritual union—an opening of ourselves to receive from God—an act that gives God pleasure and plants within us the desires of our Lord.

OUTSIDE THE ARK

Let's look at the Ark's exterior. It was basically an ornate gold box with a beautiful covering called the Mercy Seat. The top and bottom, two unique, individual components, together made one complete entity—perhaps another example of the marriage union, husband and wife becoming one.

In the Holy Place, we see the presence of cherubim. Beneath the Tabernacle's skin covering, beneath the blood covering, beneath the hair covering, beneath the angelic spiritual covering, two golden angels stood guard over the place of God's presence.

Note the angels, though situated face-to-face, were not looking at each other. They looked continually to the Mercy Seat—the place blood was sprinkled and the place that united God and men.

We won't take the time to study cherubim in detail, but here's a bit of information: Cherubim are angelic beings who live in the spiritual realm. They represent righteous government, that justness of God's nature again—and they execute God's judgment. It is good for us they are looking down to the blood and not to our offenses as we enter the Holy of Holies. Hebrews 9:5 calls these angels the "cherubim of glory." There is some kind of connection between cherubim, glory and intimacy.

Most Christians have a general understanding that Jesus fulfilled the prophecies of messianic redemption, but do we really understand His plan to bring the earthly shadow of the Tabernacle in the wilderness into the heavenly realm of relationship with Him? Do we grasp the example God established in the husband-wife relationship? The gift of marriage reveals God's desire for intimacy between Christ and His bride, the Church. You see, **Heaven isn't really our destination. Jesus is.**

The Tabernacle of Moses evolved over time to David's tabernacle followed by Jerusalem's temples. The tent David established was his favorite refuge, and in his tabernacle, David reclined and worshipped before the Ark of the Covenant. As we observe the changes in worship over time, we learn to grow in our relationship with God—to linger and love and listen to His heartbeat in the same way King David exhibited—in a way that delighted the heart of God.

When David first brought the Ark of the Covenant to Jerusalem, he followed the high priest's example and removed his kingly garments in the presence of the Lord. He danced in worship before his King. David's tabernacle was a place of true worship, and an example for us to follow today. Stripped of anything we could offer God from our world, completely dependent upon His love, open, trusting and prostrate before the King of Glory, we give ourselves to God...all in the presence of angels.

INSIDE THE ARK

In the Old Testament two Hebrew words were translated "ark." The first ark is defined as a vessel of some sort and also specifically referenced Noah's ark and Moses' ark (basket). The second meaning for ark is a chest, like a money chest or coffin, and refers directly to the Ark of the Covenant. Although the words are different, scholars believe they are related. Noah's ark was said to be shaped like a chest, and it certainly held treasure—the remnant of God's great work of creation floating in a wooden vessel.

In contrast to the Old Testament, every New Testament reference to ark translates from the same Greek word that includes Noah's ark and the Ark of the Covenant. Is there a connection between these arks? Is there something more?

The New Testament Church has been called "the ark of salvation." The Greek word for church means "the called out," and that certainly parallels with Noah's ark, Moses' ark and the Ark of the Covenant. How, you wonder? In each ark there is a "calling out" and a "calling in."

"The longsuffering of God waited in the days of Noah, while the ark was a preparing, wherein few, that is, eight souls were saved by water. The like figure whereunto even baptism doth also now save us (not the putting away of the filth of the flesh, but the answer of a good conscience toward God,) by the resurrection of Jesus Christ" (1 Peter 3:20b-21).

This passage says Noah's ark is in "like figure" or similar to baptism and turning toward God with a repentant heart by the power of the resurrection of Jesus. That sounds pretty close to Acts 2:38 to me.

"And in the ark thou shalt put the testimony that I shall give thee. And there I will meet with thee, and I will commune with thee from above the mercy seat, from between the two cherubims which are upon the ark of the testimony, of all things which I will give thee in commandment unto the children of Israel" (Exodus 25:21b-22).

As God called Noah out of his world and into the ark, He calls Christians today out of the world and to Himself. No longer restricted to a chest in a tent, men and women worldwide have the awesome opportunity to turn directly to Jesus, the meeting place of deity and humanity. The physical body of Jesus was a tabernacle, a dwelling place, for the Spirit of Almighty God—like the Tabernacle in the wilderness where the Lord met with men above the Mercy Seat.

Let's take a look inside the Ark of the Covenant. The Ark held three items, and each item relates to Jesus. First mentioned were the tablets containing the Ten Commandments—a physical representation of the Word of God given to Moses.

"In the beginning was the Word, and the Word was with God, and the Word was God" (John 1:1). Note the use of capital letters that indicate Word is a proper name. Verse 3 of the same chapter tells us the Word is a "him"—the Him Who created the world.

"And the Word was made flesh, and dwelt among us, (and we beheld his glory, the glory as of the only begotten of the Father,) full of grace and truth" (John 1:14).

Undeniably, Jesus is represented in the tablets. We learn how to relate to God and man through revelation of the Word. It is through the Word we learn how to love God and others purely, without perversion—holy, without hypocrisy.

The second item in the Ark, Aaron's rod, was also a type of Christ in two aspects: 1) Jesus is identified as our High Priest (Hebrews 3:1), and 2) a budding stick of dead wood speaks to God's power over death exhibited in the resurrection of Jesus.

The rod represented priestly authority. The Church of Jesus Christ has been given authority to operate in His name. We can speak His name and command spiritual forces. We've been given the power to bind demons and dispatch angels in His name. The budding rod also displayed God's power to bring new growth into our lives, the lives of others, our churches and our communities. It is a symbol of resurrection power.

The third item, manna, literally means "what is it" and "portion." It is the food that sustained the Israelites in the wilderness and is also considered a type of Christ. As every child of God ate manna in the desert, so must every Christian partake of the Bread of Life, the body of the Lord Jesus, the one Who preserves us in our deserts and will see us safely into our Promised Land. Manna was the provision of God for His people, and Jesus is the provision of God for our world today.

I know it's symbolic, but I believe the Lord would have us **join Jesus inside the Ark's golden vault.** In my mind, I see the Ark as a type of royal litter—a bed or couch, covered and curtained— stationery at times, and at other times carried with golden poles on the shoulders of men. It is a place that is both prominent and secluded, and one prepared with much attention to detail—that all things would be ready when the King takes His bride.

As a father prepares for his son's wedding day, happy for the moment he and his betrothed will enter the inner chamber and become one, our Father delights when we "lift the lid of the Ark of the Covenant" and "join His Son Jesus inside." When we are one with Jesus, we are one with the Father, His plan since before the foundation of the world (Ephesians 1:4).

The Ark is a great place to be. When we join Jesus there, we gain what is His. A wife in good standing with her husband shares ownership of what belongs to him, and **when we are "in the Ark" with Jesus, we share in the power of His Word, His priestly authority, His resurrection power and miraculous provision.** It's all in Jesus. Isn't that exciting? It is to me, but more than all the wonderful gifts we receive when we partner with the Lord, the most important benefit of the relationship is the relationship. It's in the Ark of the Covenant we have a deep, penetrating personal connection with God.

IN CHRIST

The Ark of Moses' Tabernacle was the vehicle God used when He established covenant relationship with the Israelites. He used Noah's ark in his generation, and Moses' ark of rushes to preserve him and bring him into covenant. The covenant participants had to "get in the Ark." This Old Testament symbolism foreshadowed new things to come.

How do we apply this to our lives? **"Getting in the Ark" is a phrase I use for becoming one with Jesus—it's what happens when we are "in Christ."** Just wait until you read about the wonders of being "in Christ."

- God was "in Christ" – 2 Corinthians 5:19
- The love of God is "in Christ" – Romans 8:39
- We are sanctified "in Christ" – 1 Corinthians 1:2
- We are new creatures "in Christ" – 2 Corinthians 5:17
- We sit in heavenly places "in Christ" – Ephesians 2:6
- The godly live "in Christ" – 2 Timothy 3:12
- The promise of life is "in Christ" – 2 Timothy 1:1
- Salvation is "in Christ" – 2 Timothy 2:10
- Our liberty is "in Christ" – Galatians 2:4
- The dead that will be raised died "in Christ" – 1 Thessalonians 4:16
- We triumph "in Christ" – 2 Corinthians 2:14

- The saints and faithful brethren are "in Christ" – Colossians 1:2
- Peace belongs to those who are "in Christ" – 1 Peter 5:14
- God's eternal purpose is "in Christ" – Ephesians 3:11
- We are God's workmanship, created "in Christ" – Ephesians 2:10
- In time, God will gather all things that are "in Christ" – Ephesians 1:10

I want to be "in Christ"...that I might be among those things gathered in by God. The New Testament uses the words "in Christ" 74 times, not including the verses that say "in Him." Let's look at a verse that particularly relates to God's covenant, the Tabernacle, and being "in Christ."

"And this I say, that the covenant, that was confirmed before of God in Christ, the law, which was four hundred and thirty years after, cannot disannul, that it should make the promise of none effect" (Galatians 3:17).

This verse was a stopper for me. I looked it up in several different translations before I found some clarity in the *Geneva Study Bible*. "And this I say, that the covenant, that was confirmed before of God {which pertained to Christ} in Christ, the law, which was four hundred and thirty years after, cannot disannul, that it should make the promise of none effect."[22] This passage means that the law given to Moses did not void or replace the covenant God made with Abraham. God's promise to Abraham was one confirmed 430 years before the giving of the law which was given because of transgressions (Galatians 3:19). The promise pertained to, or was in relation or reference specifically to, the promised messiah, Jesus Christ (Galatians 3:16). God's covenants do not nullify previous agreements, but build on one another, line upon line, here a little and there a little, and all pertain to Christ, the original promise to Abraham and his descendants, including the Gentiles engrafted into his family tree.

Christians today don't meet the Lord in a literal, physical Ark. We are blessed to have access to intimacy with God in the person of

Jesus. This is one reason I don't think it's a coincidence the Ark of the Covenant has been hidden from public view since before 586 B.C.

"Behold, the former things are come to pass, and new things do I declare: before they spring forth I tell you of them" (Isaiah 42:9). God has done a new thing. **The Ark was a stepping stone from God's covenant with Adam and Eve to its fulfillment by Jesus.** With the passage of time, the seed of promise grew. With the maturation of His bride, the Lord expanded her understanding of relationship and also her call to intimacy. He did this over time as He built upon His covenants.

The Lord's beloved, the daughter of Zion, grew. The Law became her tutor. She developed through the implementation of worship under David's reign and through the teachings of Jesus—all which built upon the foundation of faith and relationship established in the covenants God made with His people.

When Jesus came, the ceremonial laws were no longer necessary for relationship. The promised Savior offered direct contact to God through Him—in Him. He made a way to repair the breach caused by sin through His death and resurrection. We can now dwell in Him (John 6:56). We abide in Him (John 15:5). In Him we live, and move and have our being (Acts 17:28). We are become the righteousness of God in Him (2 Corinthians 5:21). He chose us before the foundation of the world that we should be holy and blameless before Him in love (Ephesians 1:4). And we can know for certain that we dwell in Him and He dwells in us because He has given us His Spirit (1 John 4:13).

SIDE NOTE: Some orthodox religions teach that Jesus' mother, Mary, was the New Testament Ark of the Covenant. I understand the premise, that she was overshadowed by the Most High and carried the seed of God in her womb, but I believe there is still a literal golden Ark of the Covenant somewhere hidden in the bowels of the Earth in which it was made. With the advent of Jesus, the Ark of the new covenant is a person—Jesus.

One of the last Old Testament references to the Ark of the Covenant was made in Jeremiah. "And it shall come to pass, when ye be multiplied and increased in the land, in those days, saith the LORD, they shall say no more, The ark of the covenant of the LORD: neither shall it come to mind: neither shall they remember it; neither shall they visit it; neither shall that be done any more" (Jeremiah 3:16). It seems the prophet is speaking about the times after Jesus' coming, perhaps the time the people of God rule and reign in New Jerusalem. Regardless of the time being discussed, the point is this: in the future a physical Ark will not be in the forefront of people's thoughts or a central part of worship.

With all this in mind, the end from the beginning, it's still important to understand the concepts God gave as He built upon His covenants. He gave the Tabernacle to Moses as an example, and I want to follow the example He's given, all the while continuing to grow in knowledge and relationship.

In our quest for spiritual intimacy, to be "in Christ," we begin at the Gate. Next we stop at the Brazen Altar of repentance followed by the Brazen Laver for cleansing. We worship in the Holy Place, lighting the Candlestick, meditating at the Table of Shewbread and offering fragrant prayers on the Altar of Incense. By the time we finally enter the Most Holy Place, we are stripped of the things of this world and cleansed, brought to a place of purity and intimacy with God.

In the Ark the world is shut out, and we are shut in with our King in the place where His Spirit dwells—where the weight of His glory presses upon us as we open ourselves and give ourselves completely to Him. When we choose to enter the Ark, the secret innermost chamber of God's holy presence, we are surrounded by angels and under angelic protection. Cherubim, the guardians of God's glory, surround the Holy of Holies in its curtained walls and ceilings, a great cloud of witnesses who watch our interaction with the Lord. They watch with awe the intimacy of their Lord and His beloved, and it is sacred. It is holy.

Chapter 7

THE TABERNACLE AND 1 CORINTHIANS 11

As I studied the Tabernacle, I gained new insight into a chapter that has been the subject of a great deal of discussion over the years. In one concise chapter, 1 Corinthians 11, we find details of themes that flow throughout our study of the Tabernacle:

- divine order
- the glory of God
- angels
- communion
- prayer
- covering

When I recently read 1 Corinthians 11, I noticed a connection between long flowing hair on a woman and the second layer of the Tabernacle's coverings—the layer just after the angelic covering of the linen curtains. It was a covering made of goats' hair. I thought of how the Bible compares a woman's hair to the hair of goats, particularly in the beautiful allegory in Solomon's Song of Songs that represents the developing relationship, from courtship to consummation, between God and Israel. This relationship later conferred to Jesus and the Church, as Groom and Bride.

"Behold, thou art fair, my love; behold, thou art fair; thou hast doves' eyes within thy locks: thy hair is as a flock of goats, that appear from mount Gilead" (Song of Solomon 4:1).

SIDE NOTE: The majority of religious Jews read the Song of Solomon annually during their celebration of

Passover. The feast of Passover coincides day by day, sometimes moment by moment, with Jesus' crucifixion—the "Passion of the Christ" for His beloved.

Jesus entered Jerusalem on Palm Sunday. This was five days before His crucifixion and the same day the Jews selected the perfect male lamb for the Passover sacrifice. Many theologians believe the Last Supper Jesus shared with His disciples was actually the Passover seder meal—the same meal eaten at the first Passover in Egypt. Jesus' dying words, "it is finished" were spoken at the same time (3:00 p.m.) the priest sacrificed the Passover lamb.

On Good Friday evening, during the Feast of Unleaven Bread, first fruits grain offerings were given as a symbol that the Israelite's trusted God to provide the rest of the harvest. This coincided with Jesus' burial as He was planted in the earth—the "first fruits of those raised from the dead" (1 Corinthians 15:20). These are amazing connections to the first Passover celebrated before Moses led the people of God from Egyptian bondage to freedom.

COVERING AND AUTHORITY

The covering referenced in 1 Corinthians 11 was a sign of authority, and a woman's appropriate covering revealed she was under authority—her husband's, father's or guardian's. Being under authority has its advantages, among them, protection and provision. When a woman is under authority, in right relationship, she has power on her head—not her physical head, but her head as in her authority figure.

But what does that mean; to have power on her head? The word "on" in the phrase "on her head" in verse 10 could be translated "of position."[23] **The woman has power of position when she is in her God-ordained place.** For a married woman it is the beautiful position of a bride, not a groom. For a young single woman, her position is under her father's or guardian's authority. The position of widows, divorcees and emancipated daughters varies, depending on their situations and circumstances,[24] but regardless of the current status of a man or woman, accepting with joy our roles in God's Kingdom is an example the Church is supposed to display to the world that they might understand their relationship with God—as His beloved bride. It is the example given in the Garden, when Eve was created for Adam—not as a subservient serf, but a partner to love and cherish and share life with.

When this happens—when we accept and display the Lord's example to the world—power, glory and honor are ours. For a woman, she receives the power and authority of her "head." Having access to the authority of my husband, who has access to the authority of his Head, Jesus, is a privilege and an honor not to be taken lightly. For a man, his obedience gives him access to the authority of his Head, the Lord Jesus Christ. It's a chain reaction, and I don't ever want to break the chain. Anointing and blessing flow down from the top, and if I move from beneath the covering of my spiritual head or authority, I remove myself from the path of God's anointing.

Keep in mind that **although position means power, it does not indicate a higher or lesser value.** In 1 Corinthians 11:11, the very next verse, Paul goes on to say, "Nevertheless neither is the man without the woman, neither the woman without the man, in the Lord." It looks like as far as God is concerned, men and women need each other, and this dependency creates an equal value to Him.

Ephesians 6 gives great detail on roles and relationships. After eight verses on the subject, Paul writes in verse nine there is "no respect of persons with him" (God). The Lord doesn't play favorites based on gender or role in the Kingdom. We are all His favorites, and isn't that nice?

The hair covering principle men and women are called to display on Earth (verses 4-5) without contention (verse 16) is a witness to the world we live in and to the angels (verse 10). This covering code of conduct is for the here and now, as males and females reflect different aspects of Christ and the Church to the world. In that twinkling of an eye, when the Lord gathers all that are "in Christ" to Himself, Jesus will cover His Bride, and this example will no longer be necessary. In Heaven there is neither male or female (Galatians 3:28).

GLORY

For the here and now, God's Word says if a woman has long hair, it is a glory to her (1 Corinthians 11:15). Wow! The word *glory* in this passage is the same word translated elsewhere as the *shekinah* glory of God. We've looked at glory before, but there's more to discover. According to *Thayer's Lexicon, glory* means "a bright cloud by which God made manifest to men his presence and power on earth." [25] It also means "on whom the divine glory rests."[26]

Some argue this verse is not a direct command from the Apostle Paul. It does, after all, say, *"if* a woman has long hair." Yes, God continues to allow us our free wills. It is a woman's choice to make. But as a woman, I'm thrilled to have the opportunity and blessing, by wearing a veil of long hair, to be one "on whom the divine glory rests." Glory also means magnificence, excellence, preeminence, dignity, grace, majesty—or that which belongs to God.[27] I'd be happy with any one of those on my head.

"For a man indeed ought not to cover his head, forasmuch as he is the image and glory of God: but the woman is the glory of the man" (1 Corinthians 11:7). In direct relation to this verse, *Thayer's* says of the woman her "function and government reflects the majesty of the divine ruler because in her the preeminence and authority of her husband are conspicuous." This means **the visible, highly noticeable symbol of long hair a woman wears shows she is under her authority, which in turn gives her authority.** The woman reflects the majesty of God, the Divine Ruler, in the way she functions and governs her life. Keep in mind a lexicon is not a commentary, but a wordbook or dictionary that deals strictly with language use and vocabulary. What *Thayer's* gives us is not personal opinion on what someone thinks 1 Corinthians 11:7 means, but strictly what the language and vocabulary literally indicate.

A proper hair covering shows proper relationship. It is a recognition that woman was made for man the same way humankind was made for God—a treasured but weaker vessel—an object of love to be cherished as His bride. Accepting and celebrating our roles as men and women in God's creation brings a harmony and peace that leads to beautiful intimacy and protection. It imparts authority to those aligned with the authority over them. When a woman keeps her hair, she keeps her position, which gives her power. When a man cuts his hair, he continues in his position, which gives him power, as well. We are examples to the world of Christ and the Church—examples I believe angels watch as surely as they watched over the Holy Place of the Tabernacle—with awe and wonder.

"The LORD thy God in the midst of thee is mighty; he will save, he will rejoice over thee with joy; he will rest in his love, he will joy over thee with singing" (Zepheniah 3:17).

God is in the midst of His people rejoicing over them. His desire is to take our hands and lead us to a place of intimacy—the secret place of the Most High. "He that dwelleth in the secret place of the most High shall abide under the shadow of the Almighty" (Psalm 91:1). God is our habitation (Psalm 91:9). We live, we abide, we dwell in safety and protection inside the Tabernacle with Him. It's the result of a conscious choice—to choose God and His ways—to set our affections on things above (Colossians 3:2). Bishop G.A. Mangun put it this way: "Being hid in God guides my affections."[28] It keeps us from being exposed to the affections of the world that would draw us away from relationship with God.

"How amiable are thy tabernacles, O LORD of hosts" (Psalm 84:1). God's dwelling place is lovely. It is the place of communion, the final subject covered in the jam-packed chapter of 1 Corinthians 11. How quickly we turn to the end of the chapter to partake of communion with the Lord and skip over the beginning. We must be in right relationship before we partake of the Lord's communion. We are called to "judge ourselves" (verse 31) and "examine ourselves" (verse 28) or we may eat the Lord's Supper unworthily (verse 27). Paul said that taking the Lord's Supper unworthily was the very reason many were weak, sick and even dead (verse 30).

DIVINE ORDER

The principles of 1 Corinthians 11 were very important to Paul. He began the chapter asking the members of the Corinthian church to be followers of him as He followed Christ (verse 1)—to follow His leadership and teaching as he received it from God—like Moses gave the teaching of God to the Israelites in the wilderness. In the second verse he admonished the Church to keep the ordinances he gave them, followed by all the points we just discussed. He concludes the chapter saying, "And the rest will I set in order when I come" (verse 34). Paul, the "Apostle of the Gentiles" (which would include most of us reading this book), considered these issues weighty matters—things that could not wait until he could speak to them in person, but instead he urgently addressed them in the most expedient manner of the day.

Let's look a bit further into the passage. "Neither was the man created for the woman; but the woman for the man. For this cause ought the woman to have power on her head because of the angels" (1 Corinthians 11: 9-10).

Here's another Scripture that says "for this cause" in reference to male-female relationships. What's the cause? God's established order. And what should we do for the cause? Be covered. Why? To have power and because of the angels. Let's break that down.

Woman was made for man, and when she willingly submits to God's plan and shows that in the way she respects her distinct function and role, her long hair reveals on the outside the acceptance of God's divine order and authority structure. By her conduct, of her own free will, she has power on her head. The Greek word for power, *exousia*, not only means she has a sign of her husband's authority, but a sign of regal authority, a crown. *Exousia* as used in 1 Corinthians 11 is the same word used in John 1:12: "But as many as received him, to them gave he power to become the sons of God, even to them that believe on his name."

To have authority, we must be under authority. Look at the example of the Centurion soldier in Matthew 8. This military leader understood authority because he was a man "under authority" who also had the power to command men beneath his rank. He recognized Jesus' authority came from above which gave Him power over things below. Note that military leaders must act in accordance with the desires of the government giving them power. To do otherwise would be foolish and result in discipline and possibly removal from office and loss of power. Spiritual authority follows this same pattern. We must remain under authority to act with authority and power.

ANGELS

We can't forget about the angels. There's been much confusion surrounding the four-word phrase "because of the angels." Before God ordered creation, order was already established in heaven. Of course, angels had free will, or Lucifer could not have chosen to rebel against God. But for the angels that remained loyal to God, order and obedience to authority were the way they operated. Disobedience, with the exception of Lucifer's fall with one-third of the angels, is not the way of Heaven.

Disrupting God's order is not a small thing. John Chrysostom, the Archbishop of Constantinople, in his teachings on 1 Corinthians 11, said that a woman who casts off her covering "disturbs all things and betrays the gifts of God, and casts to the ground the honor bestowed. For to [the woman] it is the greatest of honor to preserve her own rank.[29] Although many modern women abdicate their role and attempt to raise their positions, Chrysostom says in rebuttle, "She doth not mount up, but rather falls from her own proper honor. Since not to abide within our own limits and the laws of God, but to go beyond, is not an addition, but a diminuition." In other words, what she does in an attempt to raise her position, ends in a loss, not a gain.

Angels dwell within a hierarchy, and they understand authority. They don't fight for rank, but serve where they are placed. In the same way, when men and women accept their positions, angels take note. Angels are surely among the cloud of witnesses mentioned in Hebrews 12:1. Angels are everywhere. They set up camp around people who fear or reverence the Lord (Psalm 34:7). They watch over us (Psalm 91:11), and we just don't know when we might entertain angels unaware (Hebrews 13:2).

Wherever we are, we are undoubtedly in an angelic line of vision. There's glory involved with the presence of angels. I have to tell you, I don't get it all, but I'm overwhelmed by the connection I've found between covering, relationship, angels and glory.

- Angels are the guardians of God's glory.
- Angels serve as mediators between God and men.
- Angels carry our prayers before the Lord.
- Angels are witnesses to our relationships... even our most intimate ones!

I don't have Bible for this, so I give you my thoughts on the matter. The cherubim woven into the curtains of the Holy of Holies and the golden angels seated on the mercy seat speak to me of angels observing the relationship between God and men. They watched at Eden's gate as Adam and Eve were evicted from the Garden. They watched in the Holy Place of the Tabernacle, and they watch now.

Celestial attendants observe with wonder as the redeemed of the Lord enter into relationship with their King. They watch with wonder as the great romance plays out. They see the example of marriage between a husband and wife and wait with the Lord for the day He will come for His betrothed and takes her for His own.

I believe angels watch and are amazed, but I also believe they watch and are repelled when they witness blatant disobedience and rebellion to God's Word. They want the Lord they serve to be honored. They know He is holy and worthy. They understand authority. I want my conduct to invite the presence of angels into every aspect of my life, not repulse them or drive them away.

In both 1 Corinthians 11 and the Holy Place of the Tabernacle, we see angels. In 1 Corinthians 11, they watch over our prayer and seem to connect Heaven and Earth like the ladder in Jacob's dream (Genesis 28:12). Throughout Scripture, angels have served important roles between God and men.

- They serve as messengers (Daniel 10; Acts 7:52-53)
- They meet physical needs (Genesis 21:17-18; 1 Kings 19:5-6)
- They protect from danger (Daniel 3; Daniel 6) and deliver from danger (Acts 5; Acts 12)
- They minister strength and encouragement (Matthew 4:11; Acts 27:23-25)
- They are used by God to answer prayer (Daniel 9:20-24; Daniel 10:10-12; Acts 12:1-17).
- They give direction and guidance (Matthew 1:18-21; Acts 8:26)
- They care for God's people as they pass from this life to the next (Luke 16:22).

God uses angels to connect the unseen with the seen, the spiritual with the physical, needs with resolutions, weakness with strength, questions with answers. In addition to their roles as mediaries, messengers and ministers between Heaven and Earth, their main function in Heaven is to offer praise and worship to the Lord (Isaiah 6:1-3; Revelation 4).

In the Tabernacle, angelic presence and covering are represented by the cherubim woven in the linens on the walls and ceiling of the Holy of Holies and the two golden cherubim on the Mercy Seat. The angels on the Ark may well represent cherubim who protect the sacred inner sanctum in the same way cherubim were placed at the entrance to the Garden of Eden. These angels, so attentive and on guard, watch now over Heaven's Holy of Holies, the place the Lord God Almighty will rejoice over His bride.

As long as the Israelite's used Moses' Tabernacle, angels dwelt in the Holy Place. In the room and furnishings of God's own design—among coverings of tapestry, carved woodwork overlayed with gold, and fine linens of Egypt—angels watched and waited for the priest to enter on the annual Day of Atonement. They look on now, in Heaven's Holy Place, watching and waiting for the entry of the Bride of Christ—that moment the Lord will celebrate with joy and rest in His love. It will be a wonderful union in a place filled with singing and happiness and fulfillment (Zephaniah 3:17)—all in the presence of angels.

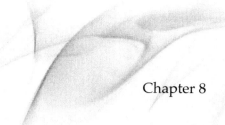

Chapter 8

THE TABERNACLE AND THE GOSPEL

We've established that the Tabernacle reveals the way to communion with God, but that's Old Testament. What about the Gospel? What about the New Testament and the New Covenant? What did Jesus have to say?

"Jesus saith unto him, I am the way, the truth, and the life: no man cometh unto the Father, but by me" (John 14:6). Jesus is **the Way, the Truth and the Life.** Let's break that down.

Jesus is:

1. *The Way*

   Like the Gate, the entryway that leads into the Tabernacle Courtyard, or the Door to the Holy Place, Jesus is the Way. "Then said Jesus unto them again, Verily, verily, I say unto you, I am the door of the sheep. I am the door: by me if any man enter in, he shall be saved, and shall go in and out, and find pasture" (John 10:7; 9). Either way, be it the outer Gate or the inner Door, **Jesus is the only entrance into the Tabernacle**, the holy Tent of Meeting.

2. *The Truth*

   Jesus, the Truth, laid out a straight path—one without curves, twists or variables, that leads from the Gate or Door into the Most Holy Place. The Pharisees and Herodians said Jesus "teachest the way of God in truth" (Mark 12:14). Paul wrote "truth is in Jesus" (Ephesians 4:21) and "Now I say that Jesus Christ was a minister of the circumcision for the truth of God, to confirm the promises made unto the fathers" (Romans 15:8). The truth of God Jesus ministered confirmed the promises given in the Old Testament, including those given to Moses at the founding of the Tabernacle.

3. *The Life*

The tent of the Tabernacle, **the Most Holy Place, is the place of Life**—a physical representation of the Holy of Holies in heaven where we will experience eternal communion with God. The Bible says we are "alive in Christ" (Romans 6:1). "For the wages of sin is death, but the gift of God is eternal life in Christ Jesus our Lord" (Romans 6:23). These verses say we are alive *in* Christ— not with Christ, not as Christ, not like Christ, but we are alive in Christ.

ORDER IN THE TABERNACLE

Note the prescribed order in John 14:6 and the correlation to the Tabernacle layout. You can't enter Life, the Most Holy Place, until you've first entered through the Way, the Gate. The Gate leads to Truth, the true path that leads to Life. Jesus' words guide us through the Old Testament Tabernacle that pointed men to Him. This Tabernacle roadmap, this infallible "heavenquest," gives the directions men and women of every generation must follow on the path to intimacy with God.

Looking at the layout and divisions of the Tabernacle, we see different levels of relationship that also speak of our salvation experience. Remember, in the New Testament, we are members of God's royal priesthood and we have access to every part of the Tabernacle.

1. Everyone begins at the beginning. We start our journeys with God in an Outer Court experience that first acknowledges Him and then connects with Him through repentance and baptism.

2. Next is the Tent of Meeting. It is here we find places of service and ministry within the Tabernacle. These develop

over time and maturity. In biblical times, being born a Levite was not enough to grant access to the Tabernacle. It was a privilege earned by training, growth and integrity.

3. By the time we pass through the Holy Place and enter the inner chamber of the Holy of Holies, our relationship with God has grown to a much deeper level. Here we commune with the One Who waits for us behind the Veil.

A few years ago I spoke at a local prayer breakfast. It was a quarterly meeting where Christians of all denominations gathered to pray for our community. Doctrinally, we had our individual convictions, but we found common ground in the validity of the Bible and Jesus as our Savior.

As I spoke, I encouraged the people to change their thinking of "community." I felt the Lord impress me that community is more than just a group of people in the same geographic region, and His purpose was not to build an organization or group. Instead of seeking to build community, I told them I believed the heart of God was that His people would "come" in "unity" before Him—to seek the Lord—His guidance, His direction. Isn't unity the Lord's goal, after all? Unity with Him and unity with each other? Isn't coming into unity what marriage is all about—the two shall become one?

Becoming one is much more than a physical act. Look at marital intimacy, the example the Lord provided of His relationship with His bride, the Church. As we see marriages disintegrate all around, it's obvious husbands and wives can "be there" in the marriage bed and not truly "be one" in their thoughts, hopes and dreams—the core and essence of their hearts, souls and spirits. **Being one with Christ is the result of giving yourself completely to Him—coming into unity with Him—with His divine love and purpose.**

ACTS 2:38

"And Peter answered them, Repent (change your views and purpose to accept the will of God in your inner selves instead of rejecting it) and be baptized, every one of you, in the name of Jesus Christ for the forgiveness of and release from your sins; and you shall receive the gift of the Holy Spirit" (Acts 2:38, AMP).

Most of us are familiar with this verse, but just look at how the *Amplified Bible* expounds on the word *repent* in the parenthetical phrase: "change your views and purpose to accept the will of God in your inner selves instead of rejecting it." On the day of Pentecost, the birthday of the New Testament Church, Peter told the people their first step in getting things right with God was to repent, and that means to:

- change your views,
- change your purpose, and
- accept the will of God in your inner selves instead of rejecting it.

These three bullet points could be summed up in the phrase "come into unity with God." The Lord wants to share His views, His purpose and His will with us—to transform us into His image (2 Corinthians 3:18). **A simple definition of repentance could be "coming into unity with God."** That's something to aim for, isn't it? And as beautiful as that is for each individual person, it's not just about us, or for us, individually. When we are with Jesus, shut in with Him, He changes us and we reflect His light to the world around us. We become living epistles, letters read among men—a primary theme of 2 Corinthians 3.

In addition to repentance, Acts 2:38 includes two more components. The three basic elements of this verse connect the Old Testament Tabernacle to God's New Testament plan of salvation in another beautiful way.

- Repentance is exemplified at the Brazen Altar of Sacrifice
- Baptism is exemplified at the Brazen Laver
- Receiving the Holy Ghost is exemplified by the indwelling presence of God in the Holy of Holies.

There are many New Testament/Old Testament connections between the Tabernacle and Jesus. Recall how the word used for *ark* in the Old Testament, the same word used for the Ark of the

Covenant, was translated "coffin" in Genesis 50:26. The Ark of the Covenant may well be an early representation of Jesus' tomb.

Consider the construction of the Mercy Seat covering the Ark of the Covenant. The top of the Ark was basically a flat plane with a cherub on either side. Now fast forward to the tomb on resurrection morning. What did Mary see when she looked inside? She "seeth two angels in white sitting, the one at the head, and the other at the feet, where the body of Jesus had lain" (John 20:12). Angels flanked the tomb, the stone slab where Jesus had lain in the same way they flanked the Ark's Mercy Seat. I love this parallel between the Mercy Seat and the tomb.

Jesus called His body the temple. "Jesus answered and said unto them, Destroy this temple, and in three days I will raise it up. Then said the Jews, Forty and six years was this temple in building, and wilt thou rear it up in three days? But he spake of the temple of his body" (John 2:19-21).

Jesus spoke these words to the Jews whose current-day temple had been patterned after the Old Testament Tabernacle with its Holy Place and Most Holy Place separated by a veil. The Greek word *naos,* translated "temple" in this verse referred specifically to the Holy Place.[30] Jesus was indeed saying His body was the very Holy Place of God. No wonder the leaders were in an uproar. How could a mere man make such a claim?

During the time Jesus walked the Earth, the Ark was not housed in the Holy Place. I find this thought-provoking. Perhaps it is no coincidence—that God would not compete with the Ark of the Covenant. It was after the Ark was hidden away or taken in battle, the Lord walked in the fleshly "tabernacle" of Jesus' physical body.

By His own blood Jesus entered Heaven's Holy Place (Hebrews 9:12), but where was the Mercy Seat on that great Day of Atonement? Perhaps it was the garden tomb itself, as the Ark represented, or perhaps there are more mysteries to uncover.

Chapter 9

COVERING AND INTIMACY

Like so many excellent teachers, God uses visuals. He gave His people the Tabernacle, the visual place of His dwelling, to reveal His plan for spiritual indwelling. Jesus used parables in His teachings—examples in the natural that gave insight into the spiritual. Like a parable, the Tabernacle was a physical picture of spiritual concepts.

When God gave Moses the pattern for the Tabernacle, Moses followed it exactly as God spoke it. It was an earthly example of things already established in Heaven. The Tabernacle plan, the pathway into the very presence of God, provided a place for Moses to speak intimately with the Lord. God spoke to Moses from above the Ark of the Covenant inside the Holy of Holies.

"There, above the cover between the two cherubim that are over the ark of the Testimony, I will meet with you and give you all my commands for the Israelites" (Exodus 25:22).

The Hebrew word *ya`ad*, translated "meet" in this passage means exactly what we would expect: to meet with someone or come together at an appointed place. This same word was also translated "betrothed" in Exodus 21:8-9.[31]

BETROTHAL

As God gave Moses His commands for the Israelites, could He have been writing a betrothal agreement for His bride? **Could it be that the Law was a marital contract written in love—the** terms of a wedding agreement between a Groom and His potential Bride? To understand this concept, we need to look beyond our modern understanding of engagements and explore the elements of betrothal in biblical times.

According to the *Jewish Encyclopedia* the first step of the betrothal process was the establishment of a marriage covenant initiated by a prospective bridegroom. The groom negotiated with the father of the bride-to-be and they agreed on terms. Once the groom paid the terms, the betrothed man and woman were considered husband and wife, although they did not live together or consummate their marriage for a period of time, twelve months under normal circumstances.

During their separation, the groom returned to his father's house to ready the couple's accommodations while the bride assembled her trousseau and prepared to leave her family. When the time was accomplished, and the groom was ready to receive his wife, he and his attendants made a procession to the bride's home. They usually arrived in the evening, and the men would shout so the bride would know her groom had come. She and her attendants would then quickly prepare themselves and travel back to the groom's father's house with the groom's party. Upon their arrival, the bride and groom were escorted into a private chamber where the groom removed his bride's veil and the couple consummated the marriage covenanted and paid for many months prior.

Before the veil was removed and intimacy and cohabitation began, betrothal negotiations agreed upon by the bride and groom were binding both in legal and religious matters.[32] A woman betrothed was considered a wife. (See 2 Samuel 3:14, Deuteronomy 22:24). Betrothal, or giving one's troth, was a pledge of faithfulness, fidelity and loyalty, especially related to engaging oneself to marry.[33] It was a contracted marriage, but not a completed marriage until it was consummated.

Before the veil of the Holy Place ripped at the time of Jesus' death, His bride had not yet been taken to the inner chamber, but the betrothal agreement, God's covenant with His people, had already been established. The Lord bound Himself to His people—His betrothed. And in response, His betrothed agreed to His terms and bound themselves to Him in a pledge of faithfulness and loyalty.

With His Word, God wrote the betrothal contract—His covenant with men. At Calvary He paid the price and fulfilled the terms, and then returned to Heaven to prepare a place for His bride. The time will come when He will collect her, free from the veil of human flesh, and unite with her, Spirit to spirit, in intimacy.

Although this is a picture of past, present and future, remember that spiritually we have permission to operate "on Earth as it is in Heaven" in the here and now. In our flesh we can't begin to know the depths of the spiritual experiences yet to happen, but God has given us glimpses in His Word and a down payment of His Spirit (2 Corinthians 1:22) that we might taste and see that He is good and experience in this life the joy of pleasing our Lord. And as we delight ourselves in Him, He returns the joy we give Him by giving us the true desires of our hearts (Psalms 37:4). That's the beauty of living in a reciprocal relationship where both involved desire to please one another. When you plant pleasure, you reap pleasure.

Another similarity between the Tabernacle and the Jewish betrothal process involved celebrations after intimacy. Once the bride and groom entered the bridal chamber, the male attendants waited outside for the groom to announce the consummation of the marriage. After the announcement was made, a great shout went up and the banqueting and celebrating began in earnest.

Each year on the Day of Atonement the high priest entered behind the tall linen curtains of the inner chamber of the Most Holy Place to offer incense and sprinkle blood on the Mercy Seat (Leviticus 16:13-14). It was the culmination of a week of preparation and a day of ceremonial rites and sacrifices. The high priest alone presented himself in the inner chamber before the Lord. When he left the Holy of Holies, the Day of Atonement came to a close with joyous celebration. The day's fast was broken. Men and women danced in the vineyards dressed in white, and the high priest officiated over a banquet in his home.[34]

A betrothal is a type of covenant, an agreement between a man and woman to marry. Covenant partners traditionally give one another gifts. After Jesus paid the betrothal price for His Bride, His own life's blood, He took power from Satan and gave gifts to men (Ephesians 4:8). Our Groom has given much for and to His Bride. Oh, how He loves us.

When people are in covenant, the things brought into the relationship that used to be theirs individually, belong from that point on to the union they created. As the betrothed of God, the moment we accept the terms of His agreement, all that we have belongs to Him and all He has belongs to us, even before the consummation of the spiritual marriage. **We are the beneficiaries of God's gifts of love.** Why? Because we are so wonderful and irresistible? Of course not, but because God made us and He chooses to delight in us.

"Thou shalt no more be termed Forsaken; neither shall thy land any more be termed Desolate: but thou shalt be called Hephzibah, and thy land Beulah: for the LORD delighteth in thee, and thy land shall be married. For as a young man marrieth a virgin, so shall thy sons marry thee: and as the bridegroom rejoiceth over the bride, so shall thy God rejoice over thee" (Isaiah 62:4-5).

The Lord delivered the Israelites from Egypt for a reason. He wanted to be their God and He wanted them to be His people. **The day they walked out of Egypt was not the day they walked into their destination, but it was the day they walked into their destiny**—they stepped onto a predetermined course that would lead Israel, the daughter of Zion, God's wife, to Her future. But before the patient Groom took His beloved to the Promised Land, the Israelites first journeyed through the wilderness for 40 years. Forty years represents a generation, the time it takes for a new generation to rise. It is a life-span, and an example of the time we live on earth before entering into the Promised Land.

God kept the Israelites in the wilderness to reveal Himself and the path to true relationship before He fulfilled His promise to take them to their new home. He gave His young betrothed time to grow and mature.

THIS CAUSE

In the following passage, the Lord was speaking to His people living in Jerusalem. This was long after the wilderness wanderings when the people were established in their cities and homes.

"I have caused thee to multiply as the bud of the field, and thou hast increased and waxen great, and thou art come to excellent ornaments: thy breasts are fashioned, and thine hair is grown, whereas thou wast naked and bare. Now when I passed by thee, and looked upon thee, behold, thy time was the time of love; and I spread my skirt over thee, and covered thy nakedness: yea, I sware unto thee, and entered into a covenant with thee, saith the Lord GOD, and thou becamest mine" (Ezekiel 16:7-8).

A few verses later, in this same passage, the Lord calls Israel's unfaithfulness "as a wife that committeth adultery, which taketh strangers instead of her husband!" (Ezekiel 16:32). The marriage analogy just keeps on going…from Old Testament to New. "For this cause shall a man leave his father and mother, and shall be joined unto his wife, and they two shall be one flesh. This is a great mystery: but I speak concerning Christ and the church" (Ephesians 5:31-32).

What is "the cause"—the reason men and women should join together? The verse before gives the reason: "For we are members of his body, of his flesh, and of his bones" (Ephesians 5:30). I used to get confused on this matter. Are we, the Church, the Bride of Christ? Or are we the Body of Christ? The week I made a note to do a study on the topic, the answer came to me in the very next adult Sunday school class. John Broyles taught the lesson, and it really clarified this concept for me.

I'll tell you what He said, but first I want to explain where I was coming from. You might think I'm crazy, but I had a mental image of the Church as a literal body and Jesus as its head. Of course, it was figurative, but yes, in my mind, Jesus' head was sitting right on the shoulders of the Church—a spiritual body made of the souls of the saints. Aren't we His hands and feet, after all? It's an odd picture, but I was just trying to make sense of the Scripture as best I could.

At the same time I had a picture in my mind of the Bride of Christ—a composite person made up of the souls of the saints—like a physical body made up of individual atoms, the basic units of matter. I could see that. It made sense. But how could the Church be both the Body and the Bride? If the Church is the Bride of Christ and marriage is given as an example of Christ's relationship with the Church, these images could not exist together in my understanding. I was confused.

But after that Sunday school lesson I realized it does make sense, after all, when we consider these passages:

"Therefore shall a man leave his father and his mother, and shall cleave unto his wife: and they shall be one flesh" (Genesis 2:24).

"And he answered and said unto them, Have ye not read, that he which made them at the beginning made them male and female, And said, For this cause shall a man leave father and mother, and shall cleave to his wife: and they twain shall be one flesh? Wherefore they are no more twain, but one flesh. What therefore God hath joined together, let not man put asunder" (Matthew 19:4-6).

Notice the two become one flesh, one body. **The Church is the Bride of Christ, and yet at the same time, she is His Body as she unites with the Lord and they become one**—an inseparable One. We have been paid for. We belong to Jesus—every arm, hand and tooth is His, and we are called to walk worthy—to live in ways that honor and please Him (Colossians 1:10).

Think of it this way. The things my hands do reflect on my husband, because we are one—even carrying the same name. If I used my hands to steal, that would not benefit our marriage. If I used my hands to make food for the infirmed, our marriage would be blessed. The places my husband sets his feet affect the oneness of our relationship—for the good or bad—because we are one. We can strengthen our union or weaken our union by our attitudes and actions. Regardless, my hands belong to my husband and his hands belong to me. What either of us does individually represents both to the world—either a credit or a discredit (ask any politician running for office).

Husband and wife are one family, one union. Cleaving together as husband and wife is more than a physical act, it also means "to keep close, to join to, to follow closely"…and even "catch." So if you get married, you actually do make a "catch"—and hopefully you make a good one. (Smile.)

Consider this: once a man and wife marry, their bodies no longer belong exclusively to themselves. They surrender them to their spouses. "The wife hath not power of her own body, but the husband: and likewise also the husband hath not power of his own body, but the wife" (1 Corinthians 7:4)

Here's another translation:

"For the wife does not have [exclusive] authority and control over her own body, but the husband [has his rights]; likewise also the husband does not have [exclusive] authority and control over his body, but the wife [has her rights]" (1 Corinthians 7:4, AMP).

Consider the legalities of a marital union. A man and his wife are one person in the eyes of the law in regards to debt and responsibility. They are civilly responsible for one another's spending and business activities and equally responsible to see their children raised to adulthood.

The union of husband and wife is like a peanut butter and jelly sandwich. Once it's stuck together, you just can't un-stick it. Even if you tried to pull it apart, there would still be some peanut butter stuck to the jelly and some jelly in the peanut butter.

Now, just look at this verse:

"So God created man in his own image, in the image of God created he him; male and female created he them" (Genesis 1:27). I recently had the privilege of hearing Dr. David Norris speak on the issue of gender distinction. In reference to this verse, he noted that men and women carry uniquely different attributes of God. Of course, there are similarities, as well, but let me give you an example to hopefully bring a bit of clarity to this concept.

Most women are naturally more nurturing than men, and most men are naturally compelled to labor to provide food and shelter for their families. We see both attributes in God—nurturer and provider. As men and women come together in marriage, they become one, and these attributes marry into one—that "one flesh" of their marriage union.

It would be silly to think that unless men and women were forever engaged in copulation they were not "one" in the flesh. The physical union that made them one is the work of God who joined them together (Matthew 19:6), regardless if they are together in the marriage bed, across town, or around the world. They are still one because through their marriage union, God made them one.

As the Israelites wandered in the wilderness, they learned many lessons about the God who delivered them from Egypt. They learned about God's character, His guidance and provision. Through the set-up of the camp they learned God wanted to be the central figure in their lives (Numbers 2:1-34). They learned about His beautiful covering provided by His grace and mercy.

Over the centuries and millennia, Israel has grown from her childish beginnings. She has budded and matured, and I believe the Lord is coming soon to whisk His bride away. I want to be "in Christ" on the day He carries His beloved to the secret place of intimacy in Heaven's Holy of Holies.

Chapter 10

TRUE LOVE COVERS

The Bible tells us that love covers (Proverbs 10:12, 1 Peter 4:8). God is love (1 John 4:8), and love covers. Yes, I repeated myself, but I'm trying to emphasize the point that **covering is the result of love.** Let's look at some passages on covering and love.

"For the life of the flesh is in the blood: and I have given it to you upon the altar to make an atonement for your souls: for it is the blood that maketh an atonement for the soul" (Leviticus 17:11).

"Let us be glad and rejoice, and give honour to him: for the marriage of the Lamb is come, and his wife hath made herself ready. And to her was granted that she should be arrayed in fine linen, clean and white: for the fine linen is the righteousness of saints" (Revelations 19:7-8).

The Bride of Christ will be covered in fine linen fashioned from the righteousness of the saints. How can this be when the Bible says there is none righteous—no, not one (Romans 3:10)? It is only possible because Jesus provided the greatest covering of all. Our righteousness does not come by obeying the Law, but in understanding and believing that Jesus fulfilled the law (Romans 10:4). We are made righteous by Jesus—His atonement, His covering (Romans 5:19).

Attempting to be righteous on our own by living up to the Law, even if it were possible, is not enough. "But we are all as an unclean thing, and all our righteousnesses are as filthy rags; and we all do fade as a leaf; and our iniquities, like the wind, have taken us away" (Isaiah 64:6). This passage, as distasteful as it may be, actually refers to menstrual rags. We can't come before the Lord wearing garments stained with menstrual blood. Not only is it just gross to even think about, but in the time this was written, women having their monthly cycle were considered ritually unclean. Anything the menstrual flow touched was also considered unclean. (Leviticus 15:19-30). This is a strong picture given to make the point that on our own merits, we have no access to God's presence.

> SIDE NOTE: I found it interesting that menstrual blood is considered unclean, but according to *A History of the Mishnaic Law of Purities, Volume 3*, by Jacob Neusner,[35] hymeneal blood is not unclean. There's something sacred about the coming together of husband and wife that first time, the time the hymen, a physical "veil of separation" is broken and the man and woman become one.
>
> The hymen, a symbol of a woman's purity, is a mucous membrane with *membrane* being defined in reference to biology as "a thin, pliable layer of tissue covering surfaces or separating or connecting regions, structures, or organs of an animal or a plant. [36]" Note that even the hymen is called a "covering."

We can only enter the presence of the Lord when we are clothed (covered) in His righteousness. Our righteousness (apart from God) is unclean or defiled, and such things are not allowed in the presence of God.

"But of him are ye in Christ Jesus, who of God is made unto us wisdom, and righteousness, and sanctification, and redemption" (1 Corinthians 1:30).

"I will greatly rejoice in the LORD, my soul shall be joyful in my God; for he hath clothed me with the garments of salvation, he hath covered me with the robe of righteousness, as a bridegroom decketh himself with ornaments, and as a bride adorneth herself with her jewels" (Isaiah 61:10).

Rejoice, my friend! We don't have to be afraid to come boldly before the throne of grace. God has provided all we need. He will clothe us with the garment of salvation—our wedding dress—paid for by the atoning blood of Jesus.

ATONEMENT

"And Aaron shall make an atonement upon the horns of it once in a year with the blood of the sin offering of atonements: once in the year shall he make atonement upon it throughout your generations: it is most holy unto the LORD" (Exodus 30:10).

"And not only so, but we also joy in God through our Lord Jesus Christ, by whom we have now received the atonement" (Romans 5:11).

We have atonement through Jesus. In the New Testament passage in Romans, *atonement* means an exchange, adjustment of a difference, reconciliation, or restoration of favor.[37] In the Old Testament, two different words are translated *atonement*. The first means to cover over, atone for sin, make atonement for;[38] and the second means redemptions or atonements.[39]

What is atonement? That's a 50 cent word most people don't use every day. *Easton's Bible Dictionary* says, "The meaning of the word is simply at-one-ment, i.e., the state of being at one or being reconciled."[40] It goes on to clarify that "expiation (amends) has been made for sin, i.e., it is covered."[41]

Simply put, **atonement means covering and implies being "at one" with God.** Jesus gave His blood as the means to cover our sins and bring us, clothed in His righteousness, into relationship. Only the blood of Jesus has the power to reconcile God with man. Just as He did in the Tabernacle, God looks not at the sin of guilty men, but at the blood of the innocent sacrifice. The *New International Version* translates *Mercy Seat* as *Atonement Seat*. Mercy, reconciliation, and restored relationship take place within the Veil of the Holy of Holies upon the Mercy Seat or Atonement Seat of the Ark of the Covenant.

When I speak of interacting with the Tabernacle, I am speaking figuratively, of course, but also of things completed by Jesus and of things yet to come. We don't have access to the literal Holy Place and Ark made in Moses' time, but remember, those were just shadows of things already established in Heaven. And isn't it interesting that the unseen spiritual things throw shadows upon our seen physical world?

The greatest covering of all is the one Jesus provided for His Bride through His blood, but there are many levels of biblical covering to explore, as well. God's overarching concept of covering, a key concept that begins in the Garden of Eden, is one He carries into many aspects of life.

SPIRITUAL COVERING

The need for covering began with man's sin. It originated with disobedience to God's authority. Every aspect of covering goes back to this concept, for when men and women walked in purity before the Lord, there was no need for covering sin or covering nakedness. Adam and Eve and God were in right relationship. Man and woman fellowshipped with their Creator and lived in obedience under His authority. Through their disobedience they broke relationship and required covering. Their actions were like stepping out from an umbrella into howling winds and rain.

Covering is a spiritual concept. It's what happens in the Most Holy Place, between God and man, but it doesn't stop there. It works its way from the inside to the outside.

- The Mercy Seat was *covered* by cherubim.
- The high priest *covered* himself in linen garments before entering the Holy Place on the Day of Atonement
- A sacrifice was offered to *cover* the sin of the people on the Mercy Seat.
- The Tabernacle was *covered* with four levels and types of *coverings*: linen, goats' hair, rams' skins and badgers' skins.

God covers those things that are holy, precious and set a part for Him. And what happens in the innermost chamber shows up on the outermost part of the Tabernacle—*covering*.

When discussing sin, covering does not mean God chose to disregard man's iniquities. He did not, and we should not ignore or walk away from the truth—that sin must be dealt with. Atonement came at a great price—a definite, difficult action was taken in order to cover sin. Because of God's love, He covered us. Because He wanted to restore relationship with fallen man, He came to Earth in the form of man and gave His life as payment for the penalty of our sins. We won't be discussing all the whys of blood sacrifice, it is a huge study on its own, but we must acknowledge the protocol God established to remove the penalty of sins.

When we accept the covering for sin offered by our gracious Lord and Savior, Jesus Christ, we accept the restoration of authority in our lives. Adam and Eve chose to sin, but they were not at liberty to choose the consequences of their sin. Among those consequences women were placed under the authority of their husbands. The establishment of authority does not indicate a value of worth, it simply brings about order that brings peace and direction. As a woman, it's not always fun to think of being under the authority of men, but men often have the more difficult position. Suspended between having authority over and responsibility for their wives, while at the same time remaining under the authority of God, men may often find themselves in precarious positions. "But I would have you know, that the head of every man is Christ; and the head of the woman is the man; and the head of Christ is God" (1 Corinthians 11:3).

Before communion with God was broken in the Garden, we find no hierarchy of authority between men and women. Adam and Eve both walked with God in the cool of the day. We recognize Eve was made from and for Adam, but we have few of the details of their relationship. We do know that it was pure and good—until sin entered—and that is when God clearly established men in a position of authority over women.

As humanity increased on the earth, God used prophets, judges and kings as authority figures in His Kingdom. With the birth of the Church in the New Testament, the Lord gave the five-fold ministries of apostles, prophets, evangelists, pastors and teachers to represent His authority on earth (Ephesians 4:11).

AUTHORITY

God specifically commands His people to obey earthly authority (Romans 13:1; 1 Peter 2:13-14). As exhibited by Daniel's illegal prayers (Daniel 6), God's people should obey the law of the land up to the point it contradicts His Word. Note, however, Daniel was still respectful in the way he conducted himself and spoke to the king, all the while honoring God and choosing His ways above a corrupt law set in place for evil purposes.

God established authority on the earth, and in the Word, He instructs His people to respectfully comply with their employers, church leaders and civil authorities (Hebrews 13:17). Did something crawl up your spine just now? Perhaps a bit of resistance reared its head. Or did you get a rush about your God-given rights of authority and the ways you can use that power to dominate someone else and have your way? I've got to be honest—I feel the resistance, and I wrote the words. Realistically, this following authority business could get pretty harsh or gnarled into something it was never intended to be if warped people develop skewed views of leadership. Hopefully, you are dealing with people who love God just as much as you do—good folks who adhere to the collective teachings of Jesus and His example of servant leadership.

"But it shall not be so among you: but whosoever will be great among you, let him be your minister; And whosoever will be chief among you, let him be your servant; Even as the Son of man came not to be ministered unto, but to minister, and to give his life a ransom for many" (Matthew 20:26-27). Jesus had all power, but He used it to serve. He washed His disciple's feet. He broke bread and fed the hungry when He deserved the most elegant of banquets, honor and esteem. He was the only one without sin eligible to cast the first stone at the woman taken in adultery, but He withheld His judgment and offered grace. He rendered unto Caesar what was Caesar's and brought no railing accusations against those who wrongfully condemned him. Jesus put His rights of power and authority in His back pocket and spent His time serving and influencing others to minister to humanity in the same way He did.

Let's look at the umbrella concept again to help us better understand covering. Imagine a picture of three umbrellas of graduating sizes—one on top of the other in a vertical line. As far as spiritual authority goes, the smaller, first-position umbrella represents the woman. Above her, covering her and a bit larger is the next level umbrella—her husband, father or other authority if she is not married. Above the man is Christ. Now this is important: notice we are talking about umbrellas—not clubs. Umbrellas were designed to protect, not beat into submission. God's covering is a result of His love.

To choose to step out from beneath the covering of God's authority (His authority and/or the authority He has established over our lives) is to choose to step outside His protection and the path of His blessing. Remember, the need for covering began with man's sin. It originated with disobedience to God's authority. The Lord established these controls to provide order on earth, and you and I must keep in alignment with His order to keep in right relationship with Him.

If I am feeling the urge to step outside my "covering" (God's or my husband's), I should prayerfully consider my motive: what is feeding my impulse to do things my own way—and what direction is the path of my self-will leading? Of course, people are flawed creatures—and face it, we all have bad days. As the led or the leader, when I have gotten things wrong, I need to get them right. I need to get my "wet" self to an altar of repentance, under a Holy Ghost blow dryer, and let the Spirit of God breathe His warm wind of love over me—dehydrating the worldly waters disobedience allowed to drench and pollute my life. Thankfully, God has always "held my spot," and graciously restored me to my right position every time I've asked for forgiveness. It's that Tabernacle plan again—

repentance first, then an ordered approach to the presence of God.

As a result of the first sin, God covered Adam and Eve's nakedness. When Adam and Eve disobeyed and found themselves naked, they created aprons of leaves to cover their shame. Funny, even with their new clothes, they knew they were not properly covered and hid themselves. God must have felt the same way. To replace the aprons, He made them coats of skins (Genesis 3:21). Without going into a biblical exegesis on "coats," suffice it to say a coat covers a lot more than an apron. This early biblical account gives a great example for today: Man's ideas of proper attire haven't always lined up with God's.

The concept of covering can get complicated—if we attempt to complicate it. But it can also be very simple and beautiful. As we've discussed, 1 Corinthians 11 addresses hair as a covering. This type of covering, along with every other covering we've explored, also connects with authority and relationship.

"Every man praying or prophesying, having his head covered, dishonoureth his head. But every woman that prayeth or prophesieth with her head uncovered dishonoureth her head: for that is even all one as if she were shaven. For if the woman be not covered, let her also be shorn: but if it be a shame for a woman to be shorn or shaven, let her be covered" (1 Corinthians 11:4-6).

I don't know about you, but I want to be able to pray or prophesy in every situation and event I face throughout my days. The Word says a woman dishonors her head (authority) if she prays with her physical head uncovered. Verse 15 tells us specifically a woman's long hair "is a glory to her: for her hair is given her for a covering."

I can't give you all the reasons why, but the Lord, by His design, created men and women different from each other and He wants us to celebrate, honor and maintain those differences. Long hair (which means to let it grow, as in not cutting it or shortening it[42]) is one of the distinctions God has given between men and women. Verse 14 says nature itself teaches us it is a shame for a man to have long hair. There's just something peculiar about it. It's not God's design.

Unless we take the time to understand the culture and accurate meanings of the language used in 1 Corinthians 11, we can get bogged down in all the "head" and "covering" terminology. What this passage of Scripture does is provide us a picture of a basic principle of authority. The spiritual authority of man over woman God established in the Garden of Eden is played out in the physical as a woman covers herself with long hair, and a man does not. If a woman shortens her hair, she dishonors her spiritual authority. If a man grows his hair long, he dishonors his spiritual authority.

I confess. I've had a bad hair day a time or two and wondered if keeping my hair long was worth the trouble I was experiencing at the moment. After all, in 1 Corinthians 11:10, Paul said a woman "ought," not "must" have long hair.

The Greek word for ought, *opheilō,* means "to owe," "to be in debt for," or "that which is due."[43] In our free country today, Christians have the liberty to choose how or if they will serve the Lord. It is my hope and prayer that women who understand this beautiful spiritual truth will choose to offer that which is due to the Lord—what she "ought."

Long hair on a woman is a visual "amen" to her inner acceptance of God's divine order. Although we may not fully understand everything there is to know about covering, we know enough about this biblical principle that makes it worth living out in our lives. And about those "bad hair days"—I had more of them before I made the commitment to allow my hair to grow. Yes, I believe it is worth the blessing.

Chapter 11

CREATED FOR INTIMACY

U sing the Tabernacle of Moses as a visual for God-man interaction, I believe the ultimate goal, the innermost place of communion with God, is located beneath the coverings of the Holy Place. It's inside the inner chamber—not just near the Ark of the Covenant, and not sitting upon the throne of the Mercy Seat—but within the Ark itself. When I think of what it would look like to get inside the Ark of the Covenant, it gives me a mental picture of a sacred, sheltered and safe place I can spiritually connect with God.

To get inside, the Ark must be opened, and the Lord must allow us in. He shows us the way to approach through the Tabernacle layout, but in order to participate in an act of intimacy with God, we must open ourselves to Him. We must give ourselves as a bride gives herself openly to her groom.

Ok. So it's a nice picture—but a bit abstract. How can we apply that to our lives? How do we get inside the ark—to be "in Christ" as we discussed in Chapter 6? It's as simple as following the Tabernacle Plan exemplified by the high priest's passage.

✓ We repent (the Brazen Altar).
✓ We are cleansed (the Brazen Laver).
✓ We walk in His Light (the Golden Candlestick).
✓ We remember and honor our eternal covenant with Him (the Table of Shewbread).
✓ We offer sweet scents of worship and prayer (Altar of Incense).

✓ We enter the private chamber, stripped of worldliness and pretention (the Holy Place).
✓ We offer ourselves to the Lord (the Ark of the Covenant).

It is in the Ark, we give back to God the lives He has given us—scented with the fragrance of our praise and worship—the incense of our prayers. We enter clothed in pure white linen—the garment of salvation Jesus provided through His blood. The Spirit of God dwells on the Mercy Seat between the cherubim, and under its golden lid, we slip inside and allow ourselves to be open, vulnerable, and shut in with Jesus. At the same time, we are sheltered beneath the tabernacling presence of Almighty God.

Remember, our physical bodies—our lives, and the things of this world—have been left on the Brazen Altar. We no longer live for ourselves, but we are hidden *with* Christ *in* God (Colossians 3:3). We are tucked away in a safe and secret place.

"He that dwelleth in the secret place of the most High shall abide under the shadow of the Almighty" (Psalm 91:1). The word translated "secret" is the Hebrew *cether,* and in *Strong's,* the first meaning of the word is "covering."[44] To my amazement, I found the word translated "dwelleth," *yashab,* not only means to "dwell," but can also mean "to marry."[45]

So in other words, the person who dwells (or marries) in the secret (covered) place of the Most High shall abide (or remain) under the shadow of the Almighty. Further in this Psalm, we learn more about the person who makes the Lord his dwelling place.

"Because thou hast made the LORD, which is my refuge, even the most High, thy habitation; There shall no evil befall thee, neither shall any plague come nigh thy dwelling. For he shall give his angels charge over thee, to keep thee in all thy ways" (Psalm 91:9-11).

Again note the angelic presence in the dwelling place of the Lord. Toward the end of this beautiful psalm, the voice of the speaker changes to the Lord, and He says, "Because he hath set his love upon me, therefore will I deliver him: I will set him on high, because he hath known my name." *Gesenius' Lexicon* defines the word translated *love* as "to be joined to."[46]

When we, God's people, are joined to Him in the secret covered place where He dwells, oh, the beautiful promises He gives us. He will deliver us. He will set us on high. He will send angels to watch over us. He will answer us in times of trouble. He will honor us and show us His salvation.

PROTECTION AND PROVISION

When we join the Lord inside the Ark of the Covenant, shut in with Him, we are in a safe place. As we place ourselves willingly, longingly in a position of receiving and responding to God, we open ourselves to the Lord in intimacy. Our spirits are safe from harm. We abide under angelic covering—and there are awesome things in the Ark with us: the Ten Commandments, Aaron's rod and the bowl of manna.

The Ark, a vessel of God's grace and mercy, is the place our spirits dwell in relationship with Him in righteousness, authority and provision. You see, Jesus is in the Ark. He is the Word made flesh. Jesus is the budding rod of priestly authority—the branch resurrected from death to life. Jesus is the manna—the Bread of life, God's miraculous provision for His people wandering in the deserts of their lives. Don't you just love that? And there's more…

"I will abide in thy tabernacle for ever: I will trust in the covert of thy wings" (Psalm 61:4). The first definition for the word translated *covert* is—not surprisingly—covering. The word for *wings* is a term used poetically to describe covering, as well—a metaphor for care and protection. What a beautiful picture of loving security, tucked beneath the Lord's sheltering wings…and it all happens in the Tabernacle.

SPOUSAL INTIMACY

Among the many types of relationships men and women have with God, I believe we discover His true heart and desire when

97

we look to the earthly example of intimacy between a husband and wife. God used marriage as an illustration of the intimacy He wants to have with His Bride. That's Jesus and you; Jesus and me. It's a connection that is intimate and fruitful in a mutually giving relationship. There's beauty and purity and satisfaction in this wonderful union—and yes, even holiness.

In marriage, physical intimacy is only part of the relationship that brings deeper spiritual connection between husband and wife. It is, however, an integral aspect of the marital union. It's a plan that originated in the heart of God in the beginning of creation. In the same way physical intimacy consummates a marriage between husband and wife, spiritual intimacy brings oneness with God.

"Knowing" God is a term of intimacy. In Matthew 7:23, Jesus said there will come a day when men and women will stand before Him and He will say to them He never "knew them." This passage refers to people who prophesied, cast out devils and did many wonderful works in the name of the Lord. It is possible to serve a kingdom in the name of the king without being in relationship with the king. The word "knew" in Matthew 7:23 is the same word used in Matthew 1:25— Joseph "knew her not." In other words, Joseph restrained from marital relations with Mary until after she gave birth to Jesus. Marital intimacy is the example Jesus used to relate the kind of "knowing" He desires.

Well, all this sounds really cool, doesn't it? But what does it look like to be intimate with God? After all, He's a Spirit and we are human.

Remember, the physical is an example of the spiritual. We are spirits living in human bodies. Intimacy with God is not flesh-to-flesh, but a spirit-to-Spirit union.

Our English word for *intimate* derives from the Latin word *intimus* which means "inmost; most secret; most intimate."[47] In general terms, intimate relationships are interdependent; it takes two to be intimate. Intimacy is the result of repeated interactions and needs being fulfilled. Intimate relationships engage our emotions, and in our emotions we experience love at different levels. In these relationships we find companionship enhanced by mutual commitment as we care and share our lives, our goals and our affections. And in the ultimate, most intimate relationship of all, our marriages, we also experience passionate love that includes a physical union.

When we give ourselves to intimacy with God in His divine embrace, we step into the fullness of our purpose. We were created for His pleasure. Only in intimacy with God do we find true fulfillment.

The Lord wants us to choose Him. He romances His beloved and woos her with gifts. He gives fruits and flowers in their seasons. Each morning He sends sunrise greetings, and every sunset whispers sweet invitations to commune and rest in His glorious presence.

We need not fear approaching God. Knowing His holiness, some are more afraid of the His presence than His absence, but that is not His desire. Yes, we should tremble at His Word and in His presence, but if we approach the Lord in the way He has asked and with the provision He has made, there is no fear. The King invites us behind the curtains of His chamber where we come to know Him like a bride knows her husband.

Spiritual intimacy isn't necessarily "warm fuzzy feelings," although those are part of the experience. **Intimacy with God, more than just the longing and drawing close to Him, is becoming one in purpose.** What was Jesus' prayer in John 17:21? "That they all may be one; as thou, Father, art in me, and I in thee, that they also may be one in us." God has invited us behind the Veil—to boldly approach the throne of grace (Hebrews 4:16). The Lord does not want His people to be afraid to be with Him.

One thing to remember, however, is that God's fierce love and loyalty walk hand in hand with a passionate jealousy. We must remain true to the Lord. God is a jealous God (Exodus 34:14), and He does not regard lightly His betrothed sporting with another.

How are people unfaithful to an unseen God? When they embrace seen or unseen false gods. Of course, many never outrightly, obviously forsake the Lord (or at least intend to). Instead, they follow the pattern of the Israelites of old. They simply introduce new gods into the picture. They share their allegiance with other entities and interests that take inordinate amounts of time and attention away from devotion to God.

Most Christians don't set up idols in their homes, but it's often so easy to allow our affections to be consumed with other interests that can put our feet on slippery paths that lead to idolatry and addiction. Some of these are the pursuit of wealth; substance use for pleasure or escapism; sexual sin; seeking spiritual power that can lead to new age spiritualism or witchcraft; entertainment choices that elevate pop stars and sports figures to pre-eminent positions—and the most tempting false god to serve—the idol of self—"I think…I feel…I believe…I want."

God calls following after false gods unfaithfulness (1 Chronicles 5:25), harlotry (Isaiah 1:21) and whoredom (Ezekiel 23:7)—sexual terms associated with breaking or dishonouring the pure, monogamous husband-wife relationship He longs to share with His bride. I think I can understand this concept somewhat when I imagine how I would feel if my husband told me to scooch over and make room for someone else in our bed.

> SIDE NOTE: We've looked at covering and divine order in relationships. Consider this: When Moses set up the tabernacle in the wilderness the first time, he *started* with the covering of the Holy of Holies and worked his way from the inside out. This is in reverse order to the way the people of Israel approached the presence of God. Moses went from the place of communion with God to the place of ministry to His people. Moses was shut in with God to shine among men and show men the way into His presence.
>
> The last thing Moses did when he set up the Tabernacle and its Outer Court the first time was place the curtain at the entrance—the Gate the

masses entered in. After he hung the last curtain, a cloud covered the Tent of Meeting and the glory of the Lord filled the Tabernacle. The people could not go inside because they were physically unable to see in front of them for the thick presence of God. From that day forward they looked to the Tabernacle to seek God's direction—to stay or go—as He led them. The Lord God Almighty dwelt among His people in the Tabernacle, the mobile temple of the Lord.

COME

Today, we have the blessed opportunity to personally interact with God. God wants to have a relationship with us—with you and with me. It's amazing, isn't it?

God, in His mind-boggling omnipresence, has singled you out. He has His eye on you. He's listening for your footsteps as He knocks on the door of your heart saying, "Open to me, my sister, my love, my dove, my undefiled: for my head is filled with dew, and my locks with the drops of the night" (Song of Solomon 5:2). He waits for the words of your response to His invitation to know Him, "Rise up, my love, my fair one, and come away" (Song of Solomon 2:10). It's not hard to fall in love with a God like that.

As we come to know Him more and more, we long for more and more of Him. We come alive in His presence with a mixture of pulsating joy and quiet stillness of soul. There is always something new and wonderful in His presence. Each encounter is fresh and distinct, satisfying to the soul and absolutely addictive.

When God offers covenant relationship, He extends an invitation. "But with thee will I establish my covenant; and thou shalt come into the ark, thou, and thy sons, and thy wife, and thy sons' wives with thee" (Genesis 6:18). See also Genesis 7:1.

But is it for everyone? What did Jesus say? "Come…" (Revelation 3:20; 18:4).

"Arise, my love, my fair one, and come away" (Song 2:13).

Chapter 12

THE SECRET PLACE

King David, the man "after God's own heart," gives us some insight into His relationship with God in Psalm 27. Let's look at an excerpt.

"One thing have I desired of the LORD, that will I seek after; that I may dwell in the house of the LORD all the days of my life, to behold the beauty of the LORD, and to enquire in his temple. For in the time of trouble he shall hide me in his pavilion: in the secret of his tabernacle shall he hide me; he shall set me up upon a rock" (Psalm 27:4-5).

The one thing David wanted above all other pursuits, was to be with God—to live and experience the beauty of His presence. The Lord delighted in David's desires. Why? Because they were His desires, too. God wants us to dwell in the secret place of the Most High with Him. It is a secret place, which means it may be hidden from public view, but it is a place God makes available to all who seek it. The secret place in Psalm 91 is a place of protection and defense. It is the same word used in Psalm 27:5 which specifically mentions the secret place of God's Tabernacle! The Tabernacle is where the Lord hides His beloved.

Each of the following passages contains the same word translated *secret place* or *hiding place*:

"Thou art my hiding place and my shield: I hope in thy word" (Psalm 119:114).

"Thou shalt hide them in the secret of thy presence from the pride of man: thou shalt keep them secretly in a pavilion from the strife of tongues" (Psalm 31:20).

"Thou art my hiding place; thou shalt preserve me from trouble;

thou shalt compass me about with songs of deliverance. Selah" (Psalm 32:7).

The "secret place" is also referenced in the romantic Song of Songs: "O my dove, that art in the clefts of the rock, in the secret places of the stairs, let me see thy countenance, let me hear thy voice; for sweet is thy voice, and thy countenance is comely" (Song of Solomon 2:14).

The secret place of the Most High is a singular location—as unique as a snowflake or fingerprint. It is a place of intimacy exclusive to each individual—a place each soul shares communion with their God. My secret place and your secret place is a "place" like no other. It is a holy abode—a spiritual location and lifestyle that is separated from the world and all its distractions. It is a sacred connection where intimacy need not be broken by outward circumstances.

What does the New Testament say about our secret place? What we've already visited. We are "hid with Christ in God" (Colossians 3:3). Christ is in us (Colossians 1:27). Jesus saved us for intimacy. He abides in us and we abide in Him (John 15:7).

THE "CATCH"

Well, it all sounds good up until now. There's got to be a catch somewhere, doesn't there?

The path to the secret place isn't always a petal-strewn walk in the park. It's a path that comes with personal expense, trials and sacrifice. To live in the secret place, we have to die to ourselves. Remember Colossians 3:3: "For ye are dead, and your life is hid with Christ in God."

Life with Jesus is life with a resurrected Savior. That sounds great, doesn't it? But what has to happen before a resurrection? A death.

We fellowship with Christ through suffering. To really know the Lord, to have true intimacy with Him, we must die to ourselves. The Apostle Paul had these words to say:

"Yea doubtless, and I count all things but loss for the excellency of the knowledge of Christ Jesus my Lord: for whom I have suffered the loss of all things, and do count them but dung, that I may win Christ, And be found in him, not having mine own righteousness, which is of the law, but that which is through the faith of Christ, the righteousness which is of God by faith: That I may know him, and the power of his resurrection, and the fellowship of his sufferings, being made conformable unto his death" (Philippians 3:8-10).

That we might know Him—that is our aspiration, our hope, our goal—to know the Lord and be known by Him. What does that mean, to "know" God? We've discussed it in previous chapters, but let's look at this particular verse. The word translated "know" in this passage is the Greek word *ginōskō,* which means "to learn to know," "to become known," "to understand," or "to become acquainted with."[48] It is also "a Jewish idiom for sexual intercourse between a man and a woman."[49]

There is sweet suffering in relationship—an intertwining of pleasure and pain. The pearl formed inside the injured oyster. The diamond created by heat and pressure. The rose grown on a thorny stem.

Without vulnerability, without pain, we cannot experience the fullness of pleasure. Pain is God's black velvet display. It is the darkness of the Jeweler's backdrop that sets off the brilliance of the diamond resting on it. It highlights and makes more noticeable the glorious light refracting from its many facets and planes.

The Greek word for diamond, *admas,* means "untamable" and "unconquerable," and is the source of the word *adamant.*[50] Diamonds are formed under high-pressure and high-temperature conditions when temperature changes force carbon atoms deep below the earth's mantle. They are the only gems made with a single element, carbon.

Pearls are made of calcium carbonate in the mantle of a mollusk when it is intruded upon by a parasite or other assailant. The disturbed mollusk forms a pearl sac over the irritant, repeating the process over and over, which yields over time a beautiful pearl.

Notice both diamonds and pearls are the end results of pressure, heat, injury or intrusion, and they are formed beneath mantles. A mantle is something that covers. And covering is something we've talked about many times.

Consider now that carbon is one of the three primary elements that make up the human body—the other two, hydrogen and oxygen, are predominantly found in water. Carbon is the basis for all organic molecules. Like the carbon in the diamond—like the calcium carbonate in the pearl—when the carbon of our humanity is under duress and pressed beneath the mantle of the Lord, God is at work. **Beautiful, valuable things are created in the secret places of our suffering.**

It is in knowing suffering we can experience resurrection power and fellowship with Jesus who accepted the cross and its suffering for us. Jesus tasted agony that we could experience ecstasy. Through torture, He gained triumph. Through humiliation, he earned exultation. Through suffering, He harvested satisfaction.

When we experience life's pressures and tragedies—its heat and injuries, we taste what Jesus tasted. And as we fellowship with Him in suffering, as we die to ourselves and conform our lives to His in death, we gain access to the secret place of the Most High. It's mysterious—rather oxymoronish— but the way of suffering, even to the point of death, is the way to glorious resurrection—both in the life to come and in our present circumstances.

CROSS LIFE

"I have been crucified with Christ; it is no longer I who live, but Christ lives in me, and the life which I now live in the flesh I live by faith in the Son of God, who loved me and gave Himself for me" (Galatians 2:20).

When we understand the resurrection concept, we are able to look beyond trials and difficulties and set our minds above. We have died to ourselves, and our lives are now hidden with Christ in God.

Resurrection life cannot begin until carnal living dies. But the result is constant access to the secret covered place, the shelter of the Almighty, where we are safe from any enemy and sheltered in every storm. We must choose to lay our lives, our flesh upon the altar of sacrifice. We must be cleansed by the washing of the Word to enter into the covered Holy Place and engage with the Light and the Bread of Life—where our prayers mingle with incense before the Holy of Holies.

We leave our flesh on the Altar, and our spirits enter the Tabernacle to dance with the flames of the Golden Candlestick—tongues of fire undulating beneath the covers of the sacred tent. We stand before the shewbread where we recognize our spiritual lineage and membership among the chosen tribes of Israel. We offer worship before the Altar of Incense mingled with frankincense and myrrh—both aromatics harvested from trees slashed or scraped to bring forth their sap used to anoint and in rites of burial.

As I studied the process used to acquire the frankincense and myrrh, I thought of how the Bible uses trees symbolically to represent people. I wondered…**if I am a tree, are my life's wounds releasing the sap used to create the incense that mingles with my prayers before the Lord?**

True intimacy is a sweet mingling of pleasure and pain. The word *passion* means not only compelling emotion and desire, but also suffering.[51] Consider the phrase "the passion of the Christ." It was Jesus' great love, His passion for us, that led Him down the Via Dolorosa—the way of suffering, the way of the cross.

Chapter 13

THE TREE OF LIFE

When we have a true passion for God, we will turn from the temptations of the world and no longer desire to eat from the tree of the knowledge of good and evil—looking to ourselves and seeking after knowledge that lifts our souls to haughtiness. Instead we will choose to eat daily from the tree of life.

Adam and Eve lost their opportunity to partake of the tree of life by allowing themselves to be distracted by Satan. We can't allow ourselves to be beguiled or confused—to allow lesser concerns to keep us from the most important things of eternal life. Our affections should be set on the things above, not the things of Earth. Jesus must be our passion, our desire.

Eve was deceived. She was caught between the simplicity of devotion to God and seeking knowledge and power for herself. That was the major issue concerning the two trees. One offered an uncomplicated life with God; while the other offered independence from God—a different type of knowledge, wisdom and food than what God had provided.

One of the primary tactics used by our spiritual enemy—from the Garden of Eden to today—is to trick us into losing our focus on the simplicity of devotion to God. He attempts to turn our attention away from the Lord and spotlight something else—a "tree" that complicates and distracts us from simple fellowship with God.

When I say we must "eat from the tree of life," I am of course speaking figuratively. What I am trying to convey is that we need to internalize the Spirit of God and the fruit of His Word, not the spirit of the world and its rotten fare. When we ingest and absorb the spiritual nature of God, we reveal an invisible Savior to our visible world. We embrace His Kingdom, His purposes, the will of God on Earth as it is in Heaven. We endure the work of the cross in our lives so He can bring resurrection life into our spirits. We turn from self-centered living and embrace Him—becoming wholly His.

I've heard some say Jesus is the tree of life, but I believe the cross is that tree—that tree that bears fruit and leaves for the healing of the nations like Aaron's dead rod bursting forth buds of new life. If the cross is the tree of life, consider these concepts:

- The way of the cross, though foolishness to those who don't believe, is the power of God to them that are saved (1 Corinthians 1:18).
- The chastening of the cross bears fruit—the fruit of the righteousness of God (Hebrews 12:11).
- The cross is hope fulfilled (Proverbs 11:30).
- The cross is wholesome words that lead to life (Proverbs 15:4).
- The way of the cross will bring victory and provide access to Heaven's tree of life (Revelation 2:7).

When we choose the cross, our tree of life, over the tree of the knowledge of good and evil, we are freed from being ruled by our own desires for knowledge and power—free from being ruled by selfish, self-centered souls. Instead we are governed by the mind of Christ in us—teaching us the way we should go and His will for our lives. Access to Heaven's tree of life is for those who "do his commandments" that they may enter in through the gates of the city (Revelation 22:14).

You've heard, I'm sure, Heaven's gates referred to as the "pearly gates." The Bible says that each gate is made of one large pearl. And as we've already covered, pearls are the result of opposition. Pearls are formed in defense of intrusion, assault or pain—perhaps the result of a "cross" you must bear (Matthew 16:24). Although each of us experiences our own unique circumstances, **your trials and pressures may be creating the very gate God uses to bring you before His throne.**

ROMANS 8:28

Now it's time to share one of my favorite verses.

"And we know that all things work together for good to them that love God, to them who are the called according to his purpose" (Romans 8:28).

What does this verse have to do with intimacy with God through the Tabernacle plan? The Greek word *kata*, translated "according"[52] in this verse occurs 482 times in the New Testament but was rendered many different ways by King James' translators. Most of the translations are prepositions—like "at," "among," "against," etc., but *kata* generally denotes motion or an order from a higher to a lower.

What got my attention is the Greek word *prothesis*. In Romans 8:28, this word translated "purpose"[53] is the same word translated "showbread" in three different New Testament passages. The Old Testament Tabernacle was a shadow of the heavenly and a representation of the dwelling place of God on Earth yet to come— the body of Jesus. The Table of Shewbread used in the wilderness Tabernacle was the place the priests made continual contact with God and gave a foreshadowing of communion with Jesus.

So let's look at Romans 8:28 in light of this information—in another "Lori Wagner Amplified Version" interpretation:

"And we know that all things work together for good to them that love God, to them who are called from higher (from God in Heaven) to lower (to men on Earth) to His communion table."

God, Who is higher, calls men, who are lower, to His communion table. When we eat the bread and drink the cup, our spirits unite with Him. It's a physical act that reveals a spiritual coming together, a joining in intimacy, like the marriage union of husband and wife that also symbolizes a spiritual union.

TABERNACLING WITH GOD

Jesus came to Earth with the express purpose of becoming the true Tabernacle and Sanctuary of the Living God. In Jesus we find all the elements of the Tabernacle God used to show men the plan of salvation. The Old Testament points to salvation in Jesus, and the Book of Acts walks us through the process—beginning with the birth of the Church on the Day of Pentecost (Acts 1-2).

Spirit-filled believers have access to a tremendous, dynamic relationship with God. Not only does the Spirit of God live inside us, but at the same time, we are covered with an overshadowing presence of God. **We have God's Spirit leading us, guiding our spirits in the way we should go, while all the while we are hidden in the secret place with God in Christ.** This is what I call "tabernacling with God" and it's the way I want to live my life.

Tabernacling can be explained in a type of formula that links an internal activity of God to an outward activity of God. It's extremely empowering and exciting. We are:

- Directed + Disguised
- Compelled + Concealed
- Ordained + Obscured
- Piloted + Protected
- Shepherded + Shrouded
- Steered + Secreted

Add it all together and you get one great sum:

Indwelling God
+ Overshadowing Protection
= a Holy Ghost directed and authorized saint
  with absolute liberty and power to
  follow God's direction because they are
  hidden in the secret place—
  beyond the sight or reach of their adversaries.

I once heard a preacher speak on abiding "under the shadow of the almighty." He said if we live under the shadow of God, we are in a place of complete protection and safety. After all, who can pull up a shadow—much less the shadow of God—and reach what is hidden underneath its intangible figure?

As we live in the realities of this tabernacling relationship, we are free to follow the leading of the indwelling Spirit—to do and become all God wants us to do and be. We are safe to follow His direction because at the same time He internally points the way and speaks to our hearts, we are hidden in the secret place of His protection. We are safe from any adversary. What can stop the people of God who are led by His Spirit and covered by His sheltering wings? What mountains could we move? What enemies could we defeat? What fruit could flourish in our lives? What wonders might we witness?

I don't know about you, my friend, but I think God wants us to have it all—and if that's what He wants, that's what I want. I believe it can happen, but it comes with a price. **To have all God wants for our lives, we must give our all to Him.** When we do that, when we shut ourselves in with God, we will shine among men and accomplish His will in the earth. We can occupy the "land" He's given us as we wait for the shout of our Bridegroom coming to take His betrothed unto Himself forever. And then, what a day, glorious day that shall be.

APPENDIX A: THE TENT OF DAVID

I hope you've enjoyed our exploration of the Tabernacle of Moses. Before we conclude, let's take a look at another important tabernacle in Scripture: the Tabernacle of David.

After years of struggling, the Lord gave David rest from his enemies. He no longer roamed, stalked by an oppressor, living in hiding from King Saul and his men. David, now king, lived in a beautiful cedar house. It didn't sit right with him that he should live in such finery while the ark of God was housed in curtains.

More than 400 years prior to David's time, God commanded Moses to build the Tabernacle in the wilderness. He gave meticulous, detailed instructions for this Tabernacle (Exodus 25:8-9), and as far as I know, never asked for any upgrades or renovations. Perhaps the Lord preserved the skins of the Tabernacle in the same way He kept the Israelite's clothes and shoes in the desert (Nehemiah 9:21).

The mobile Tabernacle had been a perfect fit for the Israelites in the wilderness, but once the kingdom was finally established and secure in Jerusalem, David wanted to create a permanent dwelling place for the Lord. There was just something in David's heart that compelled him to acknowledge God's holiness and sovereignty and honor Him with a beautiful house of His own. With this offering, made in gratitude and reverence, David hoped to give something special to the Lord Who had done so much for him, but what was God's response? It came through Nathan the prophet:

"Go and tell my servant David, Thus saith the LORD, Shalt thou build me an house for me to dwell in? Whereas I have not dwelt in any house since the time that I brought up the children of Israel out of Egypt, even to this day, but have walked in a tent and in a tabernacle" (2 Samuel 7:5-6).

Our initial reaction from these verses might be something like this: "Well, I guess God said the Tabernacle was what He asked for and all He wanted." But to me, it almost seems a delightful surprise to God that David wanted to honor Him by building Him a house. He was the first on record to ever make such an offer. Why then did the Lord refuse his request?

"But God said unto me, Thou shalt not build an house for my name, because thou hast been a man of war, and hast shed blood" (1 Chronicles 28:3). God denied David because he was a man of war, but He did it graciously. He allowed him to contribute to the building by gathering the supplies and drawing up the plans. David gave everything to his son Solomon who built the temple after David passed the throne to him (1 Chronicles 28:11-20).

Although David's request to build the temple was denied, it seemed to touch the heart of God. In response, as outlined in 2 Samuel 7, God established a covenant with David and his house forever while the building of the temple was left for the next generation.

David continued to meet with the Lord in the tent he had previously set up in Jerusalem. In the tent David had placed one solitary furnishing—the Ark of the Covenant (2 Samuel 6:17). Priests were organized to serve in David's tent—to present burnt offerings and worship the Lord in song. Meanwhile, the Tabernacle of Moses was still in use in Gibeon, but without the Ark of the Covenant in the Holy of Holies.

It seems David wanted the presence of God with him, but realized sacrifices for sin should still be offered in the Tabernacle as outlined by God to Moses on Mount Sinai. David did not presume to cease the plan established by God, but in his desire to be close to the Lord, he added to it, or built upon it.

Why is it important to study the Tabernacle of David? I'm sure there are lots of reasons, but my two main reasons are: 1) God promised David He would establish his house forever, and 2) David's tabernacle is the tabernacle the Lord has chosen.

God did not promise to raise the Tabernacle of Moses. He said he would raise David's tabernacle. "In that day will I raise up the tabernacle of David that is fallen, and close up the breaches thereof; and I will raise up his ruins, and I will build it as in the days of old" (Amos 9:11).

On the Day of Pentecost, Peter had this to say of King David:

"Men and brethren, let me freely speak unto you of the patriarch David, that he is both dead and buried, and his sepulchre is with us unto this day. Therefore being a prophet, and knowing that God had sworn with an oath to him, that of the fruit of his loins, according to the flesh, he would raise up Christ to sit on his throne" (Acts 2:29-30).

David's house, or family, was the lineage God chose to step into humanity in the body of Jesus Christ.

DAVID'S JERUSALEM

David set up his tabernacle, his tent, in Jerusalem on Mount Moriah. To understand the significance of the location, we first need to understand the Jerusalem of David's day was much smaller than the city we know today. It sat on top of two hills or mountains: Zion to the west, and Moriah to the east.[54] The *Bible Encyclopedia* says the name Jerusalem is "in the dual form, and means 'possession of peace,' or 'foundation of peace.' The dual form probably refers to the two mountains on which it was built."[55]

Let's look at the name of the two mountains. *Zion* means "a sunny place" or "a sunny mountain"[56] and is a used not only in reference to Mount Zion, but also the City of David and Jerusalem in general. *Moriah* means "Chosen of Jehovah."[57]

Surrounding Mount Moriah and Mount Zion, later additions to the city included two hills: Bezetha, (or New City) and Akra (or Fortress), as well as the Mount of Olives. These were all annexed as part of the city prior to Jesus' time.

God has a special place in His heart for this region. It has been speculated that it is the original location of the Garden of Eden. Some believe the Tigris-Euphrates Valley is the site for the Garden, but Genesis 4:16-17 tells us Cain settled east of Eden in the Euphrates Valley. This would be in the region of current-day Iraq and would put the site of the Garden of Eden west of Iraq.

"And the LORD God formed man of the dust of the ground, and breathed into his nostrils the breath of life; and man became a living soul. And the LORD God planted a garden eastward in Eden; and there he put the man whom he had formed" (Genesis 2:7-8).

This passage indicates to me that first God made Adam, and afterwards He planted a garden east of the location of Adam's creation. This could lead us to conclude the original site of the Garden of Eden is somewhere between Israel's border on the Mediterranean Sea and Iraq—a region that includes the land where Jerusalem sits on the peaks of Moriah and Zion.

According to www.biblewalks.com, the northern entrance to the Muslim shrine on Mount Moriah, the Dome of the Rock, is named "Garden of Eden."[58] First Century historian, Josephus, wrote regarding the Jewish temple, "The area of the priests and the Holy of Holies was on the west, facing east toward the gate of Eden, the first residence of Almighty God at His creation." Both the Muslims and the Jews referred to this location on Mount Moriah as a gate or entrance to Eden.

MORE MORIAH

On Mount Moriah, Solomon built the Lord's temple according to his father David's wishes. We cannot say conclusively the exact location. The city has been torn down and rebuilt more than once. But we do know the temple was on Mount Moriah. Modern Jews call Moriah's bedrock, the solid rock under the soil of the mountain, *Even ha-Shetiyah*,[59] or "the foundation stone." This refers to the belief held by some Jews and Muslims that the world was created by God through the use of a foundation stone. They use the following reference to back their claim:

"Therefore thus saith the Lord GOD, Behold, I lay in Zion for a foundation a stone, a tried stone, a precious corner stone, a sure foundation: he that believeth shall not make haste" (Isaiah 28:16).

The belief is that the Lord laid a foundation stone at the time of creation—a corner stone to build His earthly kingdom on what would become His eternal heavenly Kingdom. Those who follow this line of thinking believe God embedded a foundation stone below the mantle of the earth's outer layer—a seed of life sent from Heaven—and from that point of fertilization, life was birthed on the planet.

When I began this study, I certainly had no idea I would be writing on this topic, but it is interesting that in 2006, N.A.S.A. scientists discovered a fundamental building block of life in the tail of a comet. Dr. Jamie Elsila, of N.A.S.A.'s Goddard Space Flight Center in Greenbelt, Maryland, said of the finding, "Glycine is an amino acid used by living organisms to make proteins, and this is the first time an amino acid has been found in a comet."[60]

I'm not saying life on our planet is the result of a comet impacting the Earth, but it is beneficial to understand the common beliefs of the Jews and Muslims both claiming rights to the "foundation stone" on Mount Moriah. I also find the recent scientific studies interesting in that they show God's creative power is unlimited in the ways He may choose to work in our universe—and perhaps even reach the hearts of some scientists and evolutionists in the process.

On the other hand, it's sad there is so much controversy over a rock—that people are focused on a hard mass of minerals and not The Rock, Christ Jesus, the tried Stone, the precious Corner Stone, our sure Foundation.

The same Hebrew term used for the bedrock of Moriah is also the name for the sacred rock housed in the center of the Dome of the Rock on Mount Moriah. *The Jewish Heritage Online Magazine* reports that "foundation stone" was understood in two ways, as:

> "'the stone (or rock) from which the world was woven' and 'the foundation stone.' Both meanings are based on the belief that the world was created from the stone located in the Holy of Holies of the temple in Jerusalem, thus forming the center of the world. This concept is closely related to the image of Jerusalem and the temple as located at the 'navel of the world.' The Holy Ark was placed on this rock."[61]

The Muslim shrine on Mount Moriah houses the rock both Jews and Muslims regard as holy—the same foundation stone. The mosque is called *Qubbat as-Sakhrah*, or The Dome of the Rock, and is believed by many to be built on the same foundation as the first and second temples. The foundation stone, also called the pierced stone, features a hole in its southeastern corner that provides access to a chamber beneath known as "the well of souls."

Before you brand me a heretic or a lunatic, let's look at what Isaiah 28:16 really means. Isaiah, the prophet who gave us our beloved verse, Isaiah 9:6, is the same author of this "foundation stone" passage. I believe these verses are linked with the same message…the message of a coming Savior. This passage was written in direct response to people who thought they could outwit God and make their own contracts with death.

"Therefore, thus said the Lord Jehovah: `Lo, I am laying a foundation in Zion, A stone – a tried stone, a corner stone precious, a settled foundation, He who is believing doth not make haste (Isaiah 28:16, YLT).

God is not talking in the past tense, so it doesn't seem to me He's speaking of a literal stone used to make the world. He said He was laying a foundation—something to build on—and those who believe and trust will not be dismayed or ashamed. The *Amplified Bible* and the *New American Standard Bible* also translate this passage, "I am laying." The *Contemporary English Version* and *The Message* paraphrase both say, "I'm laying."

God has been laying a foundation …one that I believe included the Tabernacle in the wilderness. God instituted the Tent of Meeting to fellowship with men. He began with Moses and continued in relationship with each passing generation—His ultimate destination a place of communion in the Holy of Holies with His bride. Over time, the Lord has built upon the teachings and revelations He imparted on Mount Sinai. If we don't believe that, we can't believe the New Testament is the Word of God. Note that just a few verses before Isaiah 28:16, the "foundation stone" passage, Isaiah says: "Whom shall he teach knowledge? and whom shall he make to understand doctrine? them that are weaned from the milk, and drawn from the breasts. For precept must be upon precept, precept upon precept; line upon line, line upon line; here a little, and there a little" (Isaiah 28:9-10).

You see, God had a master plan from Creation to Revelation—from before the foundation of the world (Matthew 25:34; 1 Peter 1:20; Revelation 13:8). He created a bride for Himself. Jesus paid the price for His betrothal with His blood. The "passion of the Christ" reveals God's passion for His betrothed. Jesus said, "I came to send fire on the earth, and how I wish it were already kindled" (Luke 12:49, NIV). God has a strong and compelling desire to be with His creation—a genesis that may well have begun on Mount Moriah.

JERUSALEM HISTORY

Jerusalem, according to Jewish tradition, is considered to be the ancient city of Salem, the place Abraham engaged with Melchizedek and paid a tithe (Genesis 14:18; Psalm 76:2)—perhaps even on Mount Moriah, the site Abraham offered Isaac to the Lord.

"And he said, Take now thy son, thine only son Isaac, whom thou lovest, and get thee into the land of Moriah; and offer him there for a burnt offering upon one of the mountains which I will tell thee of" (Genesis 22:2).

It was at this location, Abraham, the father of our faith, said, "My son, God will provide himself a lamb for a burnt offering" (Genesis 22:8). Scripture tell us God provided a ram, not a lamb, for Abraham's sacrifice (verse 13). I believe Abraham was speaking prophetically of One to come—the true Lamb of God who many believe was slain on the same mountain. But before we go there, let's look chronologically at Moriah's other significant events.

King David purchased a piece of Mount Moriah, Araunah's threshing floor, to set up his tabernacle. Solomon eventually built his temple on the site in 953 B.C. It was destroyed in 586 B.C., and a second temple was later built in the same location.

Was there significance in the choice of Araunah's threshing floor? Yes. When David sinned and took a census of the people, the Lord punished Israel with a plague.

"So the LORD sent a pestilence upon Israel from the morning even to the time appointed: and there died of the people from Dan even to Beersheba seventy thousand men. And when the angel stretched out his hand upon Jerusalem to destroy it, the LORD repented him of the evil, and said to the angel that destroyed the people, It is enough: stay now thine hand. And the angel of the LORD was by the threshingplace of Araunah the Jebusite" (2 Samuel 24:15-16).

I was moved to tears as I read this passage of Scripture. God, allowed 70,000 men to be destroyed in one day. In the midst of His righteous judgment, just as the angel arrived at His beloved Mount Moriah, the Lord said, "It is enough." God extended mercy to His people once again—perhaps at the very place He first lifted soil from Earth to fashion man as His companion—His future bride, the daughter of Zion. Perhaps at the same place God extended mercy to Adam and Eve—or their son, Cain. Perhaps at the site Jesus uttered the words, "It is finished" as He took His last breath on the cross.

THE WATERS OF EDEN

The Lord established one river that went out of Eden and then branched off in four directions (Genesis 2:10). Pison means "increase," Gihon means "burst forth," Hiddekel means "rapid," and Euphrates means "fruitfulness."

We don't know the name of the original river, but we know it "burst forth" from Eden, and from it, Gihon flowed. Considering the catastrophic events our earth has experienced—from Noah's Flood to the Great Rift—it's no surprise men have not been able to conclusively determine the location of the headwaters, or beginning points of Eden's rivers. They may be hidden by God Himself. We don't know if the Gihon River and Gihon Spring are from the same water source, but it seems likely they were connected and I found no evidence to prove otherwise.

Regardless, the Gihon Spring was the primary water source for Jerusalem and the place David chose to pass his throne to Solomon.

The location of Gihon Spring is important because eyewitnesses observed and recorded that the Jewish temple was built on a spring, and Gihon Spring was the only water source for five miles around Jerusalem. An Egyptian named Aristeas visted the Temple around 285 B.C. and wrote that the temple was located over an inexhaustible spring.[62] Tacitus, a Roman historian also wrote that the temple contained a natural spring that flowed from its interior.[63]

What is the significance? Revelation talks about a river of life flowing under the throne of God. "And he showed me a pure river of water of life, clear as crystal, proceeding out of the Throne of God and of the Lamb" (Revelation 22:1).

The Bible seems to indicate the river from the Garden of Eden originated in the area of Jerusalem. We know at least one of the branches, if not the main river flowing out of the Garden of Eden, was the Gihon, which apparently burst forth as a spring from beneath Solomon's temple, the location of the Ark of the Covenant and the dwelling place for the presence of God. The waters of Gihon ran near the Mercy Seat in Solomon's temple, allegedly placed on the very foundation stone the Muslims and Jews are fighting over today. However, with the location of the Gihon Spring about one quarter mile south of the Dome of the Rock, the two groups may be contending for the wrong rock or piece of real estate.

But think about this. Could it be that the mountains of Zion host the very gateway to the Garden of Eden?

"Beautiful for situation, the joy of the whole earth, is mount Zion, on the sides of the north, the city of the great King" (Psalm 48:2).

Let's look at that passage in another translation. "Beautiful [for] elevation, A joy of all the land, [is] Mount Zion, The sides of the north, the city of a great king" (Psalm 48:2, YLT). In *Young's Literal Translation*, we see that Zion *is* the "side of the north."

The elevation of Mount Zion—its height, its magnificence, especially its northern ridge, is the joy of the whole Earth! It is the joy of the great King!

"He stretcheth out the north over the empty place, and hangeth the earth upon nothing" (Job 26:7). God picked out the spot

He wanted, stretched out "the north" – possibly referring to the heavens, and hung the earth on nothing! What an incredible God.

Scripture tells us Lucifer wanted the "sides of the north" for himself. "For thou hast said in thine heart, I will ascend into heaven, I will exalt my throne above the stars of God: I will sit also upon the mount of the congregation, in the sides of the north" (Isaiah 14:13).

Think about this—no matter where you are, north is always the same direction. It is an actual place—not so with east and west. Once you start going east you keep going east unless you make a turn. The same with west. But not the north.

Sacrifices in the Tabernacle of Moses were slain on the northern part of the altar "before the Lord" (Leviticus 1:11). This makes me think Heaven, God's spiritual kingdom, is in the north—in that area God stretched out before He hung the Earth.

Some might consider the Garden of Eden the world's navel (although the city of Cuzco in Peru literally translates "navel"), but spiritually, Eden is the north, and the Lord wants to take us there.

"Ye have compassed this mountain long enough: turn you northward" (Deuteronomy 2:3).

"For promotion cometh neither from the east, nor from the west, nor from the south" (Psalm 75:6).

The word translated "promotion" in this Psalm is the Hebrew word *har*. *Strong's Concordance* defines it as a "hill," "mountain," "hill country," or "mount."[64]

"I will lift up mine eyes unto the hills, from whence cometh my help" (Psalm 121:1).

Our help comes from the hills of Jerusalem—the hills of "the north."

BEAUTIFIED GROUND

Jesus was crucified on Golgotha. Exactly where the cross was erected we can't say for certain. The city—the site of conflicts, sieges, and razing over the ages—has seen drastic changes to its terrain and buildings. The once deep valley between Mount Moriah and

Mount Zion has been filled in with ruins and rubble. The terrain has changed since biblical times, and Jews and Christians were both expelled from Jerusalem during a revolt in 130-133-A.D. With these changes, different locations have been identified as the site of the crucifixion.

The Church of the Holy Sepulchre is the traditionally held location for Golgatha—a site under the control of four different orthodox churches. Many Protestants place the location at the Garden Tomb north of the Damascus Gate. Both sites, now inside modern-day Jerusalem's walls, were outside the city walls on Mount Moriah during the time of the crucifixion. Archeological evidence indicates another likely spot for the crucifixion is the summit (skull) of Mount Moriah. If this is the correct location, and Mount Moriah itself is the "rock" or "altar" God chose for the final sin sacrifice, it would line up with the practice of offering sacrifices on the north side of the altar.

Regardless of the location, whether we can pinpoint the ground the cross was raised or not, we know our Savior was lifted up on the hills of Zion—our help that comes from the Lord, the Lord which made heaven and earth (Psalm 121:2).

Let's look again at Psalm 48:2: "Beautiful for situation, the joy of the whole earth, is mount Zion, on the sides of the north, the city of the great King." Matthew Henry, an English commentator and minister, made the following observation:

> "The earth is, by sin, covered with deformity, therefore justly might that spot of ground, which was beautified with holiness, be called the joy of the whole earth; that which the whole earth has reason to rejoice in, that God would thus in very deed dwell with man upon the earth."[65]

What beautified the ground with holiness? The blood of Jesus. As backwards as it seems, the blood poured out in a vicious beating and horrendous crucifixion is what beautified the sacred mountains of Zion, Moriah in particular.

"But in the last days it shall come to pass, that the mountain of the house of the LORD shall be established in the top of the mountains, and it shall be exalted above the hills; and people shall flow unto it. And many nations shall come, and say, Come, and let us go up to the mountain of the LORD, and to the house of the God of Jacob; and he will teach us of his ways, and we will walk in his paths: for the law shall go forth of Zion, and the word of the LORD from Jerusalem. And he shall judge among many people, and rebuke strong nations afar off; and they shall beat their swords into plowshares, and their spears into pruninghooks: nation shall not lift up a sword against nation, neither shall they learn war any more" (Micah 4:1-3).

Zion has a prophetic destiny to be the center, or capitol of God's Kingdom (Zechariah 8:7-8).

"Thus saith the LORD of hosts; I was jealous for Zion with great jealousy, and I was jealous for her with great fury. Thus saith the LORD; I am returned unto Zion, and will dwell in the midst of Jerusalem: and Jerusalem shall be called a city of truth; and the mountain of the LORD of hosts the holy mountain" (Zechariah 8:3).

"And the Redeemer shall come to Zion, and unto them that turn from transgression in Jacob, saith the LORD" (Isaiah 59:20).

There is much to consider on the mountains of Jerusalem. Is Mount Moriah the true cradle of civilization—the Garden of Eden? Could this have been the very spot Cain slew Abel? Did Adam and Eve offer sacrifices on this mountain in the presence of cherubim guarding the entrance to the Garden of Eden?

Is Mount Moriah—the site of Abraham's sacrifice and Solomon's temple—the future seat of God's coming Kingdom? Is this bit of land—the place Jesus chose to walk during His time on Earth—the very apple of God's eye? Is this place of Christ's crucifixion the place He will come again to rule and reign in New Jerusalem with His bride?

In this place, Jesus, our precious corner stone and sure foundation, allowed Himself to be planted in a garden tomb in the Earth He created—to spring forth as a seed in rich soil with resurrection power. His resurrection from the dead caused living water to burst forth for all mankind to drink like the Gihon Spring bubbling up beneath the temple.

For me, a Gentile, one who has never walked in the Holy Land, the significance of Jerusalem and its mountains is just beginning to come to light. "But ye, O mountains of Israel, ye shall shoot forth your branches, and yield your fruit to my people of Israel; for they are at hand to come" (Ezekiel 36:8).

God spoke creation into existence. It's just the way He operates sometimes—bringing life out of rocks—existence out of barrenness—a living earth from a void universe of seemingly lifeless planets and asteroids. In the same dialogue as the last passage we read in Ezekiel, the Lord said, "And they shall say, This land that was desolate is become like the garden of Eden; and the waste and desolate and ruined cities are become fenced, and are inhabited" (Ezekiel 36:5). Jerusalem today certainly doesn't look like the lush Garden of Eden of my imaginations, but God doesn't always do things the way I imagined He did, does or will.

King David erected his tabernacle in Jerusalem. This is the place He moved the Ark of the Covenant to meet with the Lord and worship Him. At the place of God's mercy, David made a place for the Mercy Seat. And it is on Zion's mountains, God made a covenant with David to raise up and perpetuate his tabernacle, or house, forever.

After His resurrection, Jesus ascended into Heaven from Mount Olivet, a mountain outside Jerusalem during His time, and one taller than the other mountains in the city. He will return to this mountain to reign in Zion.

Zion is much more than a physical place. It is, like the Tabernacle, an earthly example of a spiritual reality. Scripture speaks of a heavenly Mount Zion.

"But ye are come unto mount Zion, and unto the city of the living God, the heavenly Jerusalem, and to an innumerable company of angels" (Hebrews 12:22).

"Then the moon shall be confounded, and the sun ashamed, when the LORD of hosts shall reign in mount Zion, and in Jerusalem, and before his ancients gloriously" (Isaiah 24:23).

God's ultimate plan is to restore Heaven and Earth—and He does it in the same way He has revealed over time. He uses a physical example to give a spiritual reality. One day He will place New Jerusalem on a new Earth, like a bride adorned for her husband (Revelation 21:2). Then He and His bride will dwell there forever, perhaps in the very site of God's original work of creation.

In that city, Jesus is the true corner stone of the foundation. "And are built upon the foundation of the apostles and prophets, Jesus Christ himself being the chief corner stone" (Ephesians 2:20).

Jesus is the Rock the Israelites drank from in the wilderness. "And did all drink the same spiritual drink: for they drank of that spiritual Rock that followed them: and that Rock was Christ" (1 Corinthians 10:4).

Jesus—not a rock on Mount Moriah—is the Pierced One. Like Adam's rib, removed to create Eve, Jesus' side was pierced for His Bride. "But one of the soldiers with a spear pierced his side, and forthwith came there out blood and water" (John 19:33-35).

He is just beautiful, isn't He? This study has further convinced me of the absolute beauty and validity of the Word of God.

The revelation of Jesus as our Savior is the rock Peter was instructed to build the church upon—not a piece of exposed bedrock on the Temple Mount. It's all about Jesus.

SPIRITUAL BIRTH IN ZION...ON ZION

It was on the mountains of Zion, possibly on Mount Moriah, the 120 disciples of Jesus met in the Upper Room on the Day of Pentecost. The exact location of the Upper Room has not been verified, but according to the information in Acts 1:13-2:41, we know it was a large room in Jerusalem near the temple and David's tomb. It was here the Church was born, witnessed by the people traveling to the temple who heard the sounds of the believers as they were filled with Holy Ghost power.

Steven, one of Jesus' disciples, called the nation of Israel God's "church in the wilderness" (Acts 7:38). Fifty days after the first Passover, this "church" arrived at Mount Sinai. Paul called 1st Century Christians the "Israel of God" (Galatians 6:16). The 1st

Century Church was established in Jerusalem fifty days after the crucifixion of Jesus, our Passover Lamb—the Lamb foretold by Abraham on the same mountain.

Now that we understand the significance of the location of David's tabernacle, let's look at some of its details and how they apply to our spiritual lives.

David set up a tent with the purpose of bringing the Ark of the Covenant into his city.

"And David made him houses in the city of David, and prepared a place for the ark of God, and pitched for it a tent" (1 Chronicles 15:1).

The Ark had been captured during a battle with the Philistines who returned it because of problems they experienced when the Ark was in their possession. They returned it to Israel where it stayed in the house of Abinadab for 20 years until King David intervened (1 Samuel Chapters 4-7).

When David, after much difficulty, fetched the Ark of the Covenant, he did not return it to the Holy Place of Moses' Tabernacle. Instead, he placed the Ark in a one-room tent where he established a radically new order of worship and communion with God.

No sin offerings were made in David's tabernacle—but burnt offerings and peace offerings, both which were voluntary. Worship took on a whole new dimension in the tent of David. He called for instruments to be used—harps, cymbals and trumpets. New songs, psalms of praise and worship, were written for this tabernacle. Instead of one high priest offering an annual sacrifice upon the secluded Mercy Seat, in David's tabernacle, special priests ministered musically before the ark continually—day and night (1 Chronicles 16).

Along with the instruments and music, David's worship, unlike the ceremonial offerings in the Tabernacle of Moses, included hand clapping and shouting (Psalm 47:1), dancing (Psalm 149:3) and waving (Psalm 134:2). There was a new kind of liberty to worship God with all kinds of instruments (Psalm 150:3-5) and banners (Psalm 20:5). In David's tabernacle, a continuous stream of people flowed in and out worshipping God before His earthly throne, the Mercy Seat.

David sat before the Lord. This is an incredible act of intimacy the priests of Moses' Tabernacle would never have engaged in. Seated before the Lord, David played and sang songs written from his heart and his own experiences with the God he loved. This is the tabernacle God wants to raise up—a tabernacle of worship, thanksgiving, offerings from the heart and intimate communication.

A Jewish wedding day is considered a personal Yom Kippur, like the Day of Atonement in which the high priest enters the Holy of Holies. When I imagine David's tabernacle, I see a picture of a Jewish *huppah*, or wedding canopy—an intimate, sanctified place. It is a place of commitment, honoring, blessing, gifting and love.

God designed the Tabernacle of Moses, but He delighted in David's tent—and the man who captured His heart. David ministered before the Lord because he loved Him. He gave out of love, wrote love songs and sang them to His Lord in their special meeting place. That's what got God's attention.

"In that day will I raise up the tabernacle of David that is fallen, and close up the breaches thereof; and I will raise up his ruins, and I will build it as in the days of old" (Amos 9:11). Through David's descendant, Jesus, God made a way for all men to experience intimacy with Him. David set the stage for the coming personal relationship available to all through Christ. God is no longer hidden or unapproachable. Everyone has access to His presence and can experience the joy of God tabernacling with men through the gift of His indwelling Spirit. "Know ye not that ye are the temple of God, and that the Spirit of God dwelleth in you?" (1 Corinthians 3:16).

"Know ye not that your bodies are the members of Christ? shall I then take the members of Christ, and make them the members of an harlot? God forbid. What? know ye not that he which is joined to an harlot is one body? for two, saith he, shall be one flesh. But he that is joined unto the Lord is one spirit" (1 Corinthians 6:15-17).

Remember how we discussed the Body and the Bride of Christ...how we are members of the Body not because we are Jesus' body, but because we are the body of His bride? Every limb, every "member" is His the same way a bride's body belongs to her husband. God wants us for Himself. He does not want a harlot, a dirty, immoral woman, a prostitute for a bride. He wants someone who is devoted to Him; who keeps herself just for His pleasure; who responds to His love with love, in love—someone who will be faithful to Him, and through their love union, become one—in holy, spiritual intimacy.

I believe David had a healthy fear of God, but in his tabernacle, free from the constraints of the Tent of Meeting in the wilderness, David communed with God in intimacy. He experienced for himself the presence of God—His mercy, His kindness, His love. David knew from personal experience that God was merciful; he knew he deserved the death penalty for his sins. Mosaic Law made no provision, no sacrifice to cover adultery or murder—and David was guilty of both. He personally experienced God's forgiveness, grace and restoration—God's amazing, unconditional love.

Yes, David was radical, but he operated with spiritual understanding.

"All this, said David, the LORD made me understand in writing by his hand upon me, even all the works of this pattern" (1 Chronicles 28:19). As David ministered, as he sat before the Lord, God wrote things in his heart, revealing His plans to His servant.

David's tabernacle ushered in a new era. He exemplified that line-upon-line, precept-upon-precept concept. David knew Solomon's temple would replace the tent he worshipped in. He knew God was coming to fulfill the covenant made with Moses (Romans 15:8; Galatians 3:17). He understood God's original plan—His desire for intimacy, but with that new understanding, He did not do away with the Tabernacle of Moses. He gave detailed instructions to Solomon on the building of the temple that incorporated the instructions given by God for the Tabernacle of Moses and new elements of worship. When construction was complete, all the furnishings of the Tabernacle in the wilderness were reunited with the Ark of the Covenant in the temple.

God's purpose, from Genesis to Revelation, book to book, unfolded through the chronologies recorded in the Word. The

Tabernacle of Moses given at Mount Sinai was established for the people of that day, and for an example for generations to come. David added precept to precept—line to line—building on the foundation laid by God.

But with all the effort David made in his preparations for the temple, it was impossible to mandate intimacy. Intimacy comes from the heart. Take a glimpse into how the Lord hurt when His Tabernacle was not set up:

"Woe is me for my hurt! my wound is grievous; but I said, Truly this is a grief, and I must bear it. My tabernacle is spoiled, and all my cords are broken: my children are gone forth of me, and they are not: there is none to stretch forth my tent any more, and to set up my curtains" (Jeremiah 2:19-20).

In another time, the Lord responded with anger and indignation; He removed His Tabernacle in judgment.

"And he hath violently taken away his tabernacle, as if it were of a garden: he hath destroyed his places of the assembly: the LORD hath caused the solemn feasts and sabbaths to be forgotten in Zion, and hath despised in the indignation of his anger the king and the priest" (Lamentations 2:6).

But even in His anger, God never forgets His covenants, and graciously, mercifully, offers restoration.

"Moreover I will make a covenant of peace with them; it shall be an everlasting covenant with them: and I will place them, and multiply them, and will set my sanctuary in the midst of them for evermore" (Ezekiel 37:26).

"And say unto them, Thus saith the Lord GOD; Behold, I will take the children of Israel from among the heathen, whither they be gone, and will gather them on every side, and bring them into their own land: And I will make them one nation in the land upon the mountains of Israel; and one king shall be king to them all...I will save them out of all their dwellingplaces, wherein they have sinned, and will cleanse them: so shall they be my people, and I will be their God.

"And David my servant shall be king over them; and they all shall have one shepherd: they shall also walk in my judgments, and observe my statutes, and do them. And they shall dwell in the land that I have given unto Jacob my servant, wherein your fathers have dwelt; and they shall dwell therein, even they, and their children, and their children's children for ever: and my servant David shall be their prince for ever. Moreover I will make a covenant of peace with them; it shall be an everlasting covenant with them: and I will place them, and multiply them, and will set my sanctuary in the midst of them for evermore. My tabernacle also shall be with them: yea, I will be their God, and they shall be my people. And the heathen shall know that I the LORD do sanctify Israel, when my sanctuary shall be in the midst of them for evermore" (Ezekiel 37:20-28).

The Lord will place us in His sanctuary, His dwelling place, forever.

God called to Moses from the Tent of Meeting (Leviticus 1:1). He met David in his tabernacle. The Lord is still calling—inviting us to enter that secret place of communion, fellowship and intimacy with Him—a place in Jesus now open to all...whosoever will...the Bridegroom says, "Come."

APPENDIX B:
WHAT HAPPENED TO THE ARK?

If you're wondering where the Tabernacle or the Ark of the Covenant are today, to my knowledge, there is no conclusive answer to this question. However, it is interesting to explore the many theories and possibilities people have offered on the subject. Before we dive into these, let's first look at what happened since the Tabernacle was erected in the wilderness.

Since the time of Moses, the Tabernacle was in use, moving with the Israelites as they wandered the desert. After the Israelites crossed the Jordan River into the Promised Land, the Tabernacle was set up in Gilgal where it stayed for 14 years as the Israelites took possession and settled in Canaan.

When the tribes were settled and the battles ended, the Tabernacle was dismantled, but its furnishings and tapestries were taken to Shiloh (Joshua 18:1) where they were used in a roofless stone sanctuary. This Tabernacle was used for 369 years until the Philistines destroyed it.

Approximately five hundred years passed between the times of Moses and David. According to David's wishes, his son Solomon built a magnificent temple that replaced the Tabernacle around 960 B.C.

The Ark of the Covenant was brought from its home in the tent set up by David and rejoined the vessels of the Tabernacle when they were transferred to Solomon's temple (2 Chronicles). The original parts of the Tabernacle in the wilderness, its beams, hooks, sockets., etc., were hidden, and their whereabouts are not public knowledge at the time of this printing.

The temple stood for around four hundred years and was destroyed by the Babylonians in 586 B.C. A second temple was built by Zerubbabel after 70 years of Jewish captivity. It was completed in 515 B.C., and expanded by King Herod the Great. Herod leveled the temple and built another, but what is referred to as Herod's temple is still considered the second temple because the offering of sacrifices continued throughout the building process. This was the temple in operation during Jesus' time.

The last time we read about the Ark of the Covenant in Scripture is in 2 Chronicles. In 623 B.C., King Josiah ordered the Ark be returned to the temple. Scholars surmise that during the reign of wicked kings or times of political threat, the Ark was removed from the temple and hidden by the priests.

Some propose the Ark was destroyed by Israel's enemies. Although it is a possibility, it doesn't seem likely. God's earthly throne could only be destroyed if He allowed it. What mere men, by their own wills and strength, could overtake and ruin something God protected? If this great calamity had occurred, it is likely it would have been mentioned in the Bible.

There is no record of the Ark being used in the second temple. History indicates the Holy Place of the second temple/Herod's temple remained empty for its near five hundred years of existence until its destruction in 70 A.D. Josephus, a 1st Century Jewish historian wrote concerning the Holy Place, "In this there was nothing at all. It was inaccessible and inviolable, and not to be seen by any; and was called the Holy of Holies."[66]

In addition to the testimony of Josephus, Roman General Pompey, who conquered Jerusalem around 63 B.C., demanded the privilege of entering the Holy of Holies. He gained entrance but exited the chamber saying he did not understand what all the interest was about—that the sanctuary was only an empty room.[67]

The *Jewish Encyclopedia* (www.jewishencyclopedia.com) records that "according to the Mishnah (Mid. iii. 6), the 'stone of foundation' stood where the Ark used to be."[68] Perhaps this is why the Jews and Muslims are in conflict over what is believed to be the foundation stone housed in the Dome of the Rock on Mount Moriah.

The foundation stone has several man-made cuts in its surface, one in particular, a flat rectangle the exact dimensions given for the Ark of the Covenant. This is believed to be the original foundation stone used in the first temple as a base for the Ark of the Covenant. In the second temple, only the rock remained in the Holy of Holies, while the Ark was safely hidden away or perhaps taken away by a conquering foe. The rock was used as a substitute by the high priest on the Day of Atonement who offered incense before it and sprinkled the blood of the sacrifices on it.

Romans destroyed the second temple in 70 A.D. Jerusalem was razed in 135 A.D., changing the landscape of the city dramatically. From a theological standpoint, it's interesting that when Jesus died and the veil of the temple ripped, the only thing in the earthly temple's Holy of Holies was a rock.

WHERE IS THE ARK OF THE COVENANT?

Some claim to know, and many theories have been bandied about, but the general public is left to its own conclusions as to the current location or existence of the Ark of the Covenant. Hypothesis and conjecture abound. Some believe it is in a church in Ethiopia yet others believe it is in a cave near the Dead Sea. The most widely accepted theory involves a secret chamber beneath the ruins of the temple.

We'll look at a few of the theories and their supporters, keeping in mind that no official Ark of the Covenant has been verified. These are very cursory overviews. If they catch your interest, any internet search engine can pull up enough information to keep you reading on the subject for weeks. I spent days on the information contained in the next few pages.

ETHIOPIA

The Ethiopian government has claimed the original Ark of the Covenant is in their possession. In order to protect the safety of the "original," copies were made and placed in other Ethiopian churches. Noted Eastern African correspondent, Graham Hancock, published a book in 1992, *The Sign and the Seal: The Quest for the*

Lost Ark of the Covenant, in which he presented his supposition that the temple was in the Saint Mary of Zion's Church in Axum, Ethiopia. I'm not a historian, but I believe it is likely the Queen of Sheba may have produced a copy of the Ark after her visit with King Solomon so she could worship his God in her country. What the Ethiopians believe to be the original Ark, may be an original copy made by the queen.

IRELAND

Irish tradition holds the Ark is buried under the Hill of Tara. It is said to be the source of the pot of gold at the end of the rainbow. Legend holds that when Jerusalem and the temple were destroyed, Jeremiah brought the Ark to Ireland and buried it in a secret tomb on Tara on the Emerald Isle.[69] Jeremiah was said to be buried in Loughcrew in 581 B.C., but there is controversy regarding this claim as no name is inscribed on the burial site, just a title that means wise sage.[70] Twentieth Century British Israelites excavated parts of the hill, but were stopped before they damaged the landmark.

ISRAEL – QUMRAN

Vendyl Jones, former Baptist Pastor turned Noahide (a monotheistic Jewish ideology based on the *Seven Laws of Noah*), believes a copper scroll discovered among the Dead Sea Scrolls is a map that pinpoints the exact location of the Ark of the Covenant. He has led eight excavations with up to three hundred volunteers in Qumran, a city located on a dry plateau near the northwestern shore of the Dead Sea in the Judean Desert. He said he would reveal the Ark to the world in August 14, 2005. Of course, that date has come and gone, but Jones, who claims to be the original "Indiana Jones" in the movie "Raiders of the Lost Ark," still hopes to reveal the Ark to the world.[71]

JORDAN – MOUNT NEBO / MOUNT PISGAH

In 2 Maccabbees 2:1-8, one of the books of the Apocrypha, Jeremiah was said to have followed a divine revelation to take the Tabernacle and Ark to Mount Nebo, the mountain Moses climbed to see the land promised to the Israelites (Deuteronomy 31:1-4). He is said to have found a cave in which he placed the Tabernacle, the Ark of the Covenant and the Altar of Incense, which he then sealed off. Hope of Israel ministries affirms that Tom Crotser, an American archeologist, has located the Ark near a monastery on Mount Nebo, also known as Mount Pisgah.[72] He reported that the Ark was found, but without its golden Mercy Seat which he believes to be in another location. Crotser did not retrieve the Ark, however, I did see a photograph of a golden box he claims to be the Ark of the Covenant at www.thefutureevent.com.[73]

JERUSALEM – SUBTERRANEAN TUNNEL OR CHAMBER

Many rabbis and biblical scholars believe the Ark of the Covenant is hidden under the ground beneath the Dome of the Rock. When Solomon built his temple, he created subterranean passages where the temple treasures, namely the golden vessels of the Holy Place, could have been hidden for protection. Rabbis Shlomo Goren and Yuhuda Getz claimed to have seen the Ark in an area Getz illegally excavated beneath the temple. When the Muslims discovered their work, threats of riots caused Israeli police to seal off the passage with reinforced concrete. The entrance is still visible from the Western Wall Tunnel.[74]

In connection with this theory, Messianic preacher, Michael Rood offers some fascinating ideas of His own. He claims that King Solomon had a marital alliance with the Egyptians who revealed the secrets of sand hydraulics used in the construction of the temple. At the entrance of the Holy Place of Solomon's temple stood two very large and hollow pillars given the names of levers. On the top of the pillars were capitals that were originally five cubits tall (1 Kings

7:16), and after an invasion were three cubits tall (2 Kings 25:14). What could have created the two cubit height difference? Rood believes chambers beneath the temple were connected to the levers and sand hydraulics were used to secret the golden furnishings to a safe place beneath the temple. The temple was subsequently destroyed, and the underground rooms and tunnels have seemingly not been entered since 586 B.C., creating a possible haven for the temple artifacts.

BENEATH GOLGOTHA

Much of Michael Rood's foundational information was provided by Ron Wyatt, an amateur archeologist who believed he actually saw the Ark of the Covenant in a most unexpected but fascinating place—hidden in a cave under the place he believed to be the site of Jesus' crucifixion.

I do need to include that the board of Wyatt Museum opted to remove this information from their website stating:

"The excavations of 2005 and 2006 at the Garden Tomb, in Jerusalem, did not completely confirm the findings as stated by the late Ronald E. Wyatt during his periods of excavation during the years 1979 to 1989. We no longer have the personal account of Ronald Wyatt to help guide us. For these reasons, until further research, the Ark of the Covenant materials presented by Wyatt Archaeological Research prior to 2005 have been removed from circulation."[75]

In the early 1880s General Charles Gordon located a site outside the old city walls he believed was the real location of Golgotha. It is in an area near a cliff that looks like a skull and has come to be called the Garden Tomb. The tomb lies beyond the Damascus Gate to the north of the temple Mount near a place called Jeremiah's Grotto. This is the area Ron Wyatt excavated and claims to have seen the Ark of the Covenant.[76]

Based on his understanding that the Ark of the Covenant likely stayed in Jerusalem within a Babylonian siege wall, he assumed it was hidden underground. What makes this all so fascinating is that he reportedly discovered a crack at the top of the chamber he believed followed the route to the place Jesus' cross was raised. The crack, lined with a dark black substance Wyatt claimed was blood, could have been the result of the quake that shook the earth at the time of Jesus' death and a direct path for the blood of Jesus to drip from Calvary's cross to the Mercy Seat hidden in the underground chamber.

It's something to think about, isn't it? The Tabernacle plan. The Passover Lamb, Jesus. The blood of the Lamb of God sprinkled on the literal Mercy Seat of the Ark of the Covenant. It wouldn't surprise me in the least.

NOTES

[1] http://www.templeinstitute.org/tabernacle.htm, March 24, 2010.

[2] Blue Letter Bible. "Dictionary and Word Search for *polis (Strong's 4172)*". Blue Letter Bible. 1996-2010. 12 Mar 2010. < http:// www.blueletterbible.org/lang/ lexicon/lexicon.cfm?Strongs=G4172&t=KJV >.

[3] Blue Letter Bible. "Dictionary and Word Search for *Ierousalēm (Strong's 2419)*". Blue Letter Bible. 1996-2010. 12 Mar 2010. < http:// www.blueletterbible. org/lang/lexicon/lexicon.cfm?Strongs=G2419&t=KJV >.

[4] Blue Letter Bible. "Dictionary and Word Search for *skēnē (Strong's 4633)*". Blue Letter Bible. 1996-2010. 12 Mar 2010. < http:// www.blueletterbible.org/lang/ lexicon/lexicon.cfm?Strongs=G4633&t=KJV >.

[5] Blue Letter Bible. "Dictionary and Word Search for *skēnoō (Strong's 4637)*". Blue Letter Bible. 1996-2010. 12 Mar 2010. < http://www.blueletterbible.org/lang/ lexicon/lexicon.cfm?Strongs=G4637&t=KJV >.

[6] Blue Letter Bible. "Dictionary and Word Search for *'ohel (Strong's 168)*". Blue Letter Bible. 1996-2010. 23 Mar 2010. < http://www.blueletterbible.org/lang/ lexicon/lexicon.cfm?Strongs=H168&t=KJV >.

[7] Mangun, G.A. "Praying Through the Tabernacle." Copyright 2007. The Pentecostals of Alexandria, Alexandria, LA.

[8] Blue Letter Bible. "Dictionary and Word Search for *skia (Strong's 4639)*". Blue Letter Bible. 1996-2010. 19 Feb 2010. < http://www.blueletterbible.org/lang/ lexicon/lexicon.cfm?Strongs=G4639&t=KJV >.

[9] Blue Letter Bible. "Dictionary and Word Search for *nĕchosheth (Strong's 5178)*". Blue Letter Bible. 1996-2010. 14 Mar 2010. < http://www.blueletterbible. org/lang/lexicon/lexicon.cfm?Strongs=H5178&t=KJV >.

[10] Blue Letter Bible. "Dictionary and Word Search for *para` (Strong's 6544)*". Blue Letter Bible. 1996-2010. 13 Feb 2010. < http://www.blueletterbible.org/lang/ lexicon/lexicon.cfm?Strongs=H6544&t=KJV >.

[11] Norris, David S., PhD. I AM: A Oneness Pentecostal Theology. Hazelwood, MO: Word Aflame Press, 2009.

[12] Blue Letter Bible. "Dictionary and Word Search for *nephros (Strong's 3510)*". Blue Letter Bible. 1996-2010. 14 Mar 2010. < http://www.blueletterbible. org/lang/lexicon/lexicon.cfm?strongs=G3510 >.

[13] Barton, Carlin A. Roman Honor: The Fire in the Bones. Berkley and Los Angeles, CA: University of California Press, 2001, page 205.

[14] Ibid.

[15] Blue Letter Bible. "Dictionary and Word Search for *tachash (Strong's 8476)*". Blue Letter Bible. 1996-2010. 14 Mar 2010. < http://www.blueletterbible.org/lang/lexicon/lexicon.cfm?Strongs=H8476&t=KJV >.

[16] Orr, James, M.A., D.D. General Editor. "Entry for 'BADGER'". "International Standard Bible Encyclopedia". <http://www.searchgodsword.org/enc/isb/view.cgi?number=T1092>. 1915.

[17] www.JewishEncyclopedia.com, 2/13/2010. < http://www.jewishencyclopedia.com/view_page.jsp?artid=662&letter=S&pid=0 >.

[18] http://www.internationalstandardbible.com/S/stacte.html, March 23, 2010

[19] Blue Letter Bible. "Dictionary and Word Search for *shĕcheleth (Strong's 7827)*". Blue Letter Bible. 1996-2010. 23 Mar 2010. < http://www.blueletterbible.org/lang/lexicon/lexicon.cfm?Strongs=H7827&t=KJV >.

[20] http://www.internationalstandardbible.com/G/galbanum.html, March 23, 2010.

[21] http://www.searchgodsword.org/lex/heb/view.cgi?number=03513, March 23, 2010.

[22] http://www.searchgodsword.org/com/gsb/view.cgi?book=ga&chapter=3&verse=27, March 23, 2010.

[23] Blue Letter Bible. "Dictionary and Word Search for *epi (Strong's 1909)*". Blue Letter Bible. 1996-2010. 16 Mar 2010. < http://www.blueletterbible.org/lang/lexicon/lexicon.cfm?Strongs=G1909&t=KJV >.

[24] Wegner, Judith Romney. Chattel or Person?: The Status of Women in the Mishna. New York. Oxford University Press, 1988.

[25] Blue Letter Bible. "Dictionary and Word Search for *doxa (Strong's 1391)*". Blue Letter Bible. 1996-2010. 23 Mar 2010. < http://www.blueletterbible.org/lang/lexicon/lexicon.cfm?Strongs=G1391&t=KJV >.

[26] Ibid.

[27] Ibid.

[28] Mangun, G.A. "Praying Through the Tabernacle." Copyright 2007. The Pentecostals of Alexandria, Alexandria, LA.

[29] Chrysostom, John and Keble, John. The Homilies of S. John Chrysostom, Archbishop of Constantinople on the First Epistle of S. Paul The Apostle to the Corinthians. Oxford, John Henry Parker, F. and J. Rivington, London, 1845.

[30] Blue Letter Bible. "Dictionary and Word Search for *naos (Strong's 3485)*". Blue Letter Bible. 1996-2010. 16 Mar 2010. < http:// www.blueletterbible.org/lang/lexicon/lexicon.cfm?Strongs=G3485&t=KJV >.

[31] Blue Letter Bible. "Dictionary and Word Search for *ya`ad (Strong's 3259)*". Blue Letter Bible. 1996-2010. 20 Feb 2010. < http:// www.blueletterbible.org/lang/lexicon/lexicon.cfm?Strongs=H3259&t=KJV >.

[32] http://www.jewishencyclopedia.com/view.jsp?artid=995&letter=B#ixzz0g6U PY7iX, February 20, 2010.

[33] "troth." *Dictionary.com Unabridged*. Random House, Inc. 20 Feb. 2010. <http://dictionary.reference.com/browse/troth>.

[34] http://www3.telus.net/public/kstam/en/temple/details/day_of_atonement.htm, February 23, 2010.

[35] Neusner, Jacob. A History of the Mishnaic Law of Purities, Volume 3. The Netherlands. E.J.Brill, Leiden, 1977.

[36] membrane. Dictionary.com. *The American Heritage® Dictionary of the English Language, Fourth Edition*. Houghton Mifflin Company, 2004. http://dictionary.reference.com/browse/membrane (accessed: February 25, 2010).

[37] Blue Letter Bible. "Dictionary and Word Search for *katallagē (Strong's 2643)*". Blue Letter Bible. 1996-2010. 25 Feb 2010. < http://www.blueletterbible.org/lang/lexicon/lexicon.cfm?Strongs=G2643&t=KJV >.

[38] Blue Letter Bible. "Dictionary and Word Search for *kaphar (Strong's 3722)*". Blue Letter Bible. 1996-2010. 25 Feb 2010. < http://www.blueletterbible.org/lang/lexicon/lexicon.cfm?Strongs=H3722&t=KJV >.

[39] Blue Letter Bible. "Dictionary and Word Search for *kippur (Strong's 3725)*". Blue Letter Bible. 1996-2010. 25 Feb 2010. < http://www.blueletterbible.org/lang/lexicon/lexicon.cfm?Strongs=H3725&t=KJV >.

[40] atonement. Dictionary.com. Easton's 1897 Bible Dictionary. http://dictionary.reference.com/browse/atonement (accessed: March 26, 2010).

[41] Ibid.

[42] Blue Letter Bible. "Dictionary and Word Search for *komaō (Strong's 2863)*". Blue Letter Bible. 1996-2010. 23 Mar 2010. < http://www.blueletterbible.org/lang/lexicon/lexicon.cfm?Strongs=G2863&t=KJV >.

[43] Blue Letter Bible. "Dictionary and Word Search for *opheilō (Strong's 3784)*". Blue Letter Bible. 1996-2010. 25 Feb 2010. < http://www.blueletterbible.org/lang/lexicon/lexicon.cfm?Strongs=G3784&t=KJV >.

[44] Blue Letter Bible. "Dictionary and Word Search for *cether (Strong's 5643)*". Blue Letter Bible. 1996-2010. 23 Mar 2010. < http://www.blueletterbible.org/lang/lexicon/lexicon.cfm?Strongs=H5643&t=KJV >.

[45] Blue Letter Bible. "Dictionary and Word Search for *yashab (Strong's 3427)*". Blue Letter Bible. 1996-2010. 23 Mar 2010. < http://www.blueletterbible.org/lang/lexicon/lexicon.cfm?Strongs=H3427&t=KJV >.

[46] Blue Letter Bible. "Dictionary and Word Search for *chashaq (Strong's 2836)*". Blue Letter Bible. 1996-2010. 23 Mar 2010. < http://www.blueletterbible.org/lang/lexicon/lexicon.cfm?Strongs=H2836&t=KJV >.

[47] http://www.myetymology.com/latin/intimus.html, February 25, 2010.

[48] Blue Letter Bible. "Dictionary and Word Search for *ginōskō (Strong's 1097)*". Blue Letter Bible. 1996-2010. 2 Mar 2010. < http://www.blueletterbible.org/lang/lexicon/lexicon.cfm?Strongs=G1097&t=KJV >.

[49] Ibid.

[50] http://www.jjkent.com/articles/diamonds-history-etymology.htm, March 24, 2010.

[51] Blue Letter Bible. "Dictionary and Word Search for *homoiopathēs (Strong's 3663)*". Blue Letter Bible. 1996-2010. 24 Mar 2010. < http://www.blueletterbible.org/lang/lexicon/lexicon.cfm?Strongs=G3663&t=KJV >.

[52] Blue Letter Bible. "Dictionary and Word Search for *kata (Strong's 2596)*". Blue Letter Bible. 1996-2010. 16 Mar 2010. < http://www.blueletterbible.org/lang/lexicon/lexicon.cfm?Strongs=G2596&t=KJV >.

[53] Blue Letter Bible. "Dictionary and Word Search for *prothesis (Strong's 4286)*". Blue Letter Bible. 1996-2010. 16 Mar 2010. < http://www.blueletterbible.org/lang/lexicon/lexicon.cfm?Strongs=G4286&t=KJV >.

[54] http://jcsm.org/StudyCenter/maps/Ancient%20Jerusalem%202.jpg, March 9, 2010.

[55] http://www.christiananswers.net/dictionary/jerusalem.html, March 24, 2010.

[56] Blue Letter Bible. "Dictionary and Word Search for *Tsiyown (Strong's 6726)*". Blue Letter Bible. 1996-2010. 24 Mar 2010. < http://www.blueletterbible.org/lang/lexicon/lexicon.cfm?Strongs=H6726&t=KJV >.

[57] Blue Letter Bible. "Dictionary and Word Search for *Mowriyah (Strong's 4179)*". Blue Letter Bible. 1996-2010. 24 Mar 2010. < http://www.blueletterbible.org/lang/lexicon/lexicon.cfm?Strongs=H4179&t=KJV >.

[58] http://www.biblewalks.com/Sites/DomeRock.html, March 8, 2010.

[59] http://www.hebrew4christians.net/Glossary/Hebrew_Glossary_-_E/hebrew_glossary_-_e.html, March 8, 2010.

[60] http://stardustnext.jpl.nasa.gov/mission/glycine.html, March 9, 2010.

[61] http://jhom.com/topics/stones/foundation.html, March 8, 2010.

[62] Aristeas, translation by Eusebius, chapter 38.

[63] Tacitus, History, Bk.5, para.12.

[64] Blue Letter Bible. "Dictionary and Word Search for *har (Strong's 2022)*". Blue Letter Bible. 1996-2010. 16 Mar 2010. < http://www.blueletterbible.org/lang/lexicon/lexicon.cfm?Strongs=H2022&t=KJV >.

[65] http://mhc.biblecommenter.com/psalms/48.htm.

[66] The Works of Josephus: New Updated Edition. Copyright 1987 by Hendrickson Publishers, Inc. pg. 707. Peabody, Massachusetts.

[67] McCall, Thomas S., Th.D. January 1997, "Levitt Letter." http://www.levitt.com/essays/ark.html 2/19/2010.

[68] http://www.jewishencyclopedia.com/view.jsp?artid=128&letter=T&search=second#ixzz0iNToCScL, March 16, 2010.

[69] http://jahtruth.net/socio.htm, March 16, 2010.

[70] http://www.biblemysteries.com/library/jeremiah.htm, March 16, 2010.

[71] http://www.jdstone.org/cr/files/noahide_fiction/vendyljones_exposed.html, March 16, 2010.

[72] http://www.hope-of-israel.org/p16.htm, March 16, 2010.
[73] http://www.thefutureevent.com/Ark.htm, March 16, 2010.
[74] http://www.templemount.org/tunnel.html, March 16, 2010.
[75] http://www.wyattmuseum.com/ac_update.htm, March 16, 2010.
[76] http://www.wyattarchaeology.com/ark.htm, March 16, 2010.